Burnout Recovery

A Guide for Freelancers to Bounce Back

(A Holistic Approach to Restoring Health and Happiness)

Jesse Younger

Published By **Tyson Maxwell**

Jesse Younger

Burnout Recovery: A Guide for Freelancers to Bounce Back (A Holistic Approach to Restoring Health and Happiness)

ISBN   978-1-998038-19-0

No part of this guidebook shall be reproduced in any form without permission in writing from the publisher except in the case of brief quotations embodied in critical articles or reviews.

Legal & Disclaimer

The information contained in this book is not designed to replace or take the place of any form of medicine or professional medical advice. The information in this book has been provided for educational & entertainment purposes only.

The information contained in this book has been compiled from sources deemed reliable, and it is accurate to the best of the Author's knowledge; however, the Author cannot guarantee its accuracy and validity and cannot be held liable for any errors or omissions. Changes are periodically made to this book. You must consult your doctor or get professional medical advice before using any of the suggested remedies, techniques, or information in this book.

Table Of Contents

Chapter 1: Recognizing Burnout

This financial disaster ought to in all likelihood appear clean, however on the contrary, it's far the most crucial step on your recovery manner. After all, in case you don't understand the way to understand or label burnout, you may now not apprehend which you have an underlying trouble within the first vicinity, and you could in no way begin your restoration journey.

Every time a person says to you, "You are a workhorse," or "I don't recognise the way you manage to do all that," despite the fact that you revel in worn-out or mentally and physical exhausted all of the time, you'll take the compliment and preserve on dwelling, hoping for subjects to get better. The sad element is that during case you don't comprehend the way to understand burnout, topics could in all likelihood in no way get higher.

So, what's burnout?

Understanding Burnout:

Its Types and Difference From Stress, Fatigue, and Exhaustion

Burnout is a nation of intellectual, physical, and emotional exhaustion probably caused by prolonged stress and fatigue. Burnout makes you revel in overwhelmed, worn-out, exhausted, and "empty inner."

Before going any similarly, do you apprehend the difference between burnout, strain, exhaustion, or fatigue? Might you be complex it with any of the three?

What is pressure?

Stress is a kingdom of emotional or intellectual stress coming from the pressure to cope with disturbing times.

For example, you could sense pressured about an upcoming mission you need to hand in or an upcoming examination. In most times, while you manipulate the annoying situation, you get once more on your everyday self.

I don't forget you presently have a better understanding of what strain is. Let us now look at fatigue and exhaustion and the manner both differ from burnout.

Fatigue and exhaustion

Fatigue refers to feeling generally worn-out or feeling consisting of you lack power. When you experience fatigued, you enjoy drowsy and worn-out. Common reasons of fatigue embody:

•Lifestyle: Poor diet regime and exercise behavior, excessive intake of alcohol, pills, or caffeine, or now not getting sufficient sleep

•Psychological: Being confused, depressed, or annoying

•Sickness

•Career or business organization: Working for prolonged shifts, doing bodily hard work, strolling for weeks in a row, losing hobby at art work, or a monotonous walking revel in.

On the other hand, exhaustion is short-lived fatigue; whilst you experience it severa instances without taking movement, you become fatigued.

In most times, resting or taking a quick break will leave you refreshed and no longer fatigued.

Having showed that you are not complicated burnout with strain, fatigue, or exhaustion, allow's test extra approximately the distinct kinds of burnout and their fundamental reasons. This will assist you understand your burnout enjoy, making it a whole lot less hard to begin your healing adventure.

Below are the commonplace types of burnout:

#: Overload Burnout

Overload burnout is the most commonplace sort of burnout. It occurs at the same time as you emerge as frantic to achieve success thru way of running more difficult and tougher, on the value of your relationships, happiness, and fitness.

Please don't misunderstand this; it's miles ok to strive for achievement. Striving to gather turns into complicated at the same time as you do no longer take a damage to take care of yourself.

For instance, what takes vicinity while you are unwell? Do you prioritize your health via taking a few time off and in search of scientific assist, or do you continue to insist on operating or analyzing? You possibly do the latter, it is why you experience burned out, right? For example, in desire to resting and giving your body time to heal, you fear about your desires and push your self to attain them, dismissing the way you revel in.

Some of the principle reasons of overload burnout are:

- Being an overachiever

If you are experiencing overload burnout, it's miles maximum probably due to the reality you're an overachiever who's in no manner glad collectively along with your success. Most of the time, you acquire greater than everybody else, but you continue to crave to carry out greater.

You in all likelihood complain of constantly working but don't recognize how or in which to prevent. You feed at the praises and popularity you acquire on your success and use that to justify your power to keep going.

Every time is paintings time; it doesn't count number if it's far for your lecturers, venture, or enterprise. And, you experience responsible when you are not walking on some thing because of the fact you diploma your honestly really worth thru your successes.

- Being a perfectionist

Perfectionists are likelier to revel in overload burnout. Perfectionism makes you remember that everything you do want to be best. To avoid making mistakes or failing, you turn out to be obsessed on your initiatives, goals, and plans.

You grow to be struggling to fulfill final dates because of the fact, in line with you, it's both you're the top notch or a failure (there can be no grey place). You over-popularity on the entirety, which leaves you swamped and harassed because of the severa pending responsibilities.

- Being a human beings pleaser

If you're a human beings pleaser, you are possibly to revel in burnout more than as quickly as due to the fact you save you at now not something to delight the people spherical you, irrespective of the fee.

You say certain to every little element people ask of you because you don't like hurting or disappointing others. This reasons you to have issues putting limitations, and additionally you switch out to be experiencing burnout because of the reality you typically generally tend to show up for absolutely everyone however you.

At the give up of the day, you go to mattress feeling mentally, psychologically, and bodily exhausted due to the fact you are taking on definitely simply anybody's troubles by means of way of performing some aspect to assist them, although it does no longer healthy your fantastic interests.

● Being competitive

When now not whatever in this international is more essential than winning, you allow not a few element or no one stand on your manner. It is wise to want to win however making the entirety a opposition is dangerous and a purpose of overload burnout.

You compete with people even as they may be no longer in competition with you. For example, if a person invitations you to a celebration, you may want to be the exceptional-dressed individual. You will skip beyond your charge variety to get the brilliant new garments and footwear available. You will spend most of some time focusing and obsessing at the party such that you can fail to address one in all a type vital duties.

You secretly desire that different human beings fail, and once they don't, you turn out to be jealous of them. You alienate the human beings you experience are doing better than you and exhaust your self for your quest to get in advance. When you win, you flow one on your subsequent competition, and the cycle keeps.

Because you've got unrealistic and vain expectancies of your self and others (in which you view special humans's "wholesome" desires, schedules, and plans as lazy or unambitious), you revel in burnout.

You grow to be exhausted and overwhelmed due to the fact in desire to playing the method and dwelling in the destiny at a time, you obsess on the product, i.E., your achievements, successes, triumph, expectancies, targets, and a success desires.

#: Neglect Burnout

Neglect burnout takes place at the same time as you enjoy demanding situations within the path of a project or an mission at art work that motives you to revel in helpless. You start doubting your competency, and with time, you locate it tough to maintain up together at the side of your responsibilities.

The most important cause of forget about burnout is imposter syndrome. Also known as perceived fraudulence, imposter syndrome is an inner enjoy that makes you experience or bear in mind you're a phony incapable of performing your duties.

You doubt yourself and sabotage your paintings because of the truth you feel like a fraud who does no longer belong or have to be wherein you're. Even with the proper qualifications, skills, revel in, abilities, and records, imposter syndrome makes you consider that your successes are due to properly fortune or different external factors.

No recollect how typically you achieve success, your notion in your self does not trade or enhance. This can make you want to do more to "make certain" no person notices how the "phony" inside you. This can bring about anxiety, pressure, tiredness, and eventual burnout.

Also, perceived fraudulence can make you passive and unmotivated, leaving you with neglected remaining dates, enormous strain, remaining-minute rushes, or unaccomplished dreams. Both of those situations are possibly to motive forget about about burnout.

#: Under-Challenged Burnout

This form of burnout takes place at the same time as you revel in underappreciated or unrecognized for your movements. It furthermore takes place while you enjoy or take into account that you have few or no opportunities to research or grow for your place of job. Hence, you lose interest, unmotivated, or cynical, which leaves you feeling like your art work life is caught.

You begin avoiding your duties at artwork and specific factors of existence. At the quit of it all, you begin feeling out of place, mentally and psychologically tired, main to burnout.

For example, when a person else continuously gets the credit score for all of the obligations you're involved in at artwork (no matter the truth which you positioned equal or more effort than them), you're in all likelihood to revel in underneath-challenged burnout.

You are also probable to enjoy underneath-challenged burnout when you have labored inside the equal function for 5-10 years without getting promoted or a beautify (regardless of the fact that you're correct at what you do). Both situations can bring about under-challenged burnout.

Chapter 2: Stages Of Burnout

We have three main types of burnout as a consequence of different factors, e.G., lack of sleep, courting pressures, economic disturbing situations, paintings strain, excessive expectations, traumatic obligations, melancholy, fatigue, isolation, and loneliness or forget of physical health.

All the ones sorts development through the equal stages.

Initially, there have been 12 tiers of burnout, however with time, researchers in this concern simplified them to the subsequent five degrees:

Stage 1:

The Honeymoon phase

Burnout can also start at the same time as you adopt a modern-day assignment, hobby, initiative, or company. Here, there are not any signs of burnout; instead, you are excited, dedicated, enthusiastic, progressive, and energetic. You have immoderate expectancies of your new challenge, and as a stop end result, you discern very difficult to be effective.

You address opportunities and obligations probable to undoubtedly effect your profession and existence. You do extra than asked of you due to the truth you observe each mission as an possibility to analyze new talents.

Even while a venture is annoying, you move the extra mile to expose your competency to your boss or clients. You studies and boom every day, and at this component, you like and revel in your art work.

You like and are free together along with your art work colleagues, boss, clients, or employees, and you are constantly happy at the identical time as at home. You are on proper terms with absolutely everyone, and for a fact, your life is ideal.

However, you can start to experience stress due to annoying and hoping that each one your plans, tasks, and goals prevail.

Although a green degree, this diploma is probably volatile. You would in all likelihood get so over excited which you forestall growing time to wind down, as a end result leading to the second one phase.

Stage 2:

Onset of pressure segment

In this degree, a few days start being more worrying than others. To manipulate and keep up, you are making your technique, commercial enterprise commercial enterprise organisation, or initiatives your primary priority, and you start developing plenty less time for your personal desires, family, and buddies.

Although although in a position, you begin noticing a number of the factors of your project which you do not like. Maybe you're underappreciated, overworked, or underneath-challenged. Maybe your boss does no longer pay your greater time bonus, or your personnel are not as efficient as you belief.

During this diploma, some of the signs and symptoms and signs and symptoms and signs and symptoms and symptoms you may start noticing are:

•Poor sound asleep behavior; at night, you warfare to go to sleep due to the reality your artwork or business business enterprise is causing you to worry and wander in idea. You nevertheless desire to attain your dreams and live up maximum of the night time time figuring out how.

•Loss of urge for meals

•Jaw ache because of teeth clenching (in the course of the day) and grinding (in a few unspecified time within the future of the night time).

- Neglecting your non-public desires

- Decreased sexual preference

- Fatigue

- Dissatisfaction on the aspect of your hobby

- Anxiety

- Avoidance

Experiencing maximum of the above signs and symptoms and signs at the equal time as present process excessive-stress tiers takes you to the third diploma.

Stage three:

Chronic pressure phase

During this stage, your standard performance and trouble-solving abilties decrease every day, inflicting you to start feeling crushed. Your efforts prevent bearing fruits as they did in advance.

You begin believing that everyone is putting an excessive amount of stress on you, and as you try and avoid this feel, you begin procrastinating. You skip over cut-off dates and objectives, and your productivity decreases.

Now that you aren't getting the acknowledgment and reward you acquired in advance, you extend a feel of failure or incompetence. You come to be sad, and due to the fact the above symptoms intensify, you begin experiencing new ones.

Some of the brand new signs and signs and signs and symptoms that could expand at some point of this level are:

•Exhaustion

You feel tired all the time, to a point where moving your muscle agencies is a trouble.

Every morning, you drag your self away from mattress no longer because of the reality you want to however due to the fact you want to. You start seeing all of your responsibilities and responsibilities at home and art work as burdens requiring you to hire all of your strength of will and energy.

•You hate your assignment

You start complaining approximately your venture, colleagues, or boss/personnel due to the fact you hate your project and every person related to the process.

You get to art work overdue and fake contamination or emergencies because of the truth you may rather be anywhere however your place of job.

You lose the inducement to complete your responsibilities, and with time, you turn out to be cynical to every responsibility that calls for hazard-taking or creativity. This turns into the begin of the journey to the demise of your profession or commercial organisation.

• You sense useless

No matter range what number of vast steps you are making at work, you sense vain at the quit of the day. This feeling receives worse at the same time as you are making mistakes, fail or obtain achievement, and don't get the credit score or reputation for it. Instead of seeking out a manner forward, you motel to feeling useless and powerless.

•Depression

It is regular to enjoy temper fluctuations from time to time. However, this regular experience becomes a problem when you begin having an in no way-ending experience of lack of interest and sadness. Yes, melancholy can reason burnout, but it could furthermore represent burnout.

So, whilst you begin feeling sad for no appropriate purpose, displeased with sports you once decided delight or joy in, and sense worthless, responsible, or experience suicidal or lack of existence mind, it'd represent that you have entered the continual stress phase.

•Memory loss

You also can begin spending an excessive amount of time on your head, wondering and thinking loads that you come to be dropping music of time. For instance, you may pass over lunch with out noticing, neglect about to drink water, or go to mattress past due truely because you acquire stuck up for your mind. You pass your skincare everyday or exercising agenda.

With time, you start experiencing reminiscence loss. The subjects that became vital to you begin slipping through your thoughts. For instance, you will probably begin forgetting your anniversaries or your dad and mom' birthdays, which you normally bear in thoughts.

•Outright rage

The amount of pressure you revel in makes you irritable with anyone and the entirety spherical you. Everyone starts offevolved offevolved getting beneath your pores and pores and skin, and you start experiencing outright rage. You sense worn-out, overwhelmed, exhausted, and worn out; therefore, you project your feelings to the humans spherical you.

•Use of alcohol, drugs, and other comforts

You can also start using alcohol and drugs like never before. You can also grow to be a drug addict or flip to extraordinary topics, e.G., immoderate TV looking, binge consuming, or dependancy to social media. You use these gadgets to distract yourself from the truth of life; the ones behavior can result in one in every of a type extreme fitness troubles.

Also, you may possibly have extended caffeine consumption as you rely upon it to maintain your self alert and lively finally of the day.

•Constant complications

Almost every day, you enjoy a headache. Although now not scientifically established how, it is amazing low fee that at the same time as you're physically and emotionally exhausted, don't get enough sleep, and abuse capsules and alcohol, you are certain to have alarming times of complications.

•Physical illnesses

Besides headaches, you're in all likelihood to experience intestine pains, pain on your intestines and belly, or tightening to your chest.

Prolonged strain and absence of sleep can motive stroke, excessive blood pressure, diabetes, kidney illnesses, and coronary coronary heart illnesses.

Stage four:

Burnout degree

Having long past thru all of the above stages and related symptoms and signs, you get to an exhaustion diploma in which it will become not possible to cope with a few thing in life (mainly your paintings). It turns into hard to have a regular life.

The continued feel of powerlessness and failure results in disillusionment and depression. You begin believing that there's no manner from your situation, and you make a decision to be detached in your responsibilities.

The present symptoms intensify, and the subsequent new ones boom:

•Feeling out of place or empty indoors

•Self- doubt

Chapter 3: Enmeshment/ Habitual Burnout Phase

During this final diploma of burnout, the signs and symptoms turn out to be embedded for your existence such that you can no longer understand them anymore.

You begin experiencing substantial ongoing physical, intellectual, and emotional fatigue. Burnout influences your profession and all components of your existence, and your energy to revel in your pastimes or even do some issue disappears.

You end up so caught within the cycle of burnout which you begin feeling very unhappy and depressed. Physical illnesses become greater encouraged and rampant due to the fact this diploma weakens your immune gadget. You may additionally start experiencing persistent anxiety and panic assault.

Although maximum human beings make a radical alternate or forestall their jobs after they hit the burnout stage—level 4—some although get to this degree. If you experience like you're already within the enmeshment phase, getting your self lower lower back to ordinary is probably very hard.

That is why, further to this manual, you will need professional psychiatry assist. Your psychiatrist will assist you conquer the signs and symptoms and signs which have become a part of your existence, on the way to be immensely beneficial to your recovery journey transferring beforehand.

Now that you have diagnosed how a long way your burnout has progressed, it's time to start your healing machine.

NOTE: Remember what we said in advance: recuperation from burnout is a adventure; it requires extra than a weekend getaway, so be affected man or woman with your self as you positioned into effect the realistic suggestions and techniques you may check from the following phase:

Recovering From Burnout

Strategic Ways to Reset and Get Back on Your Feet After Burnout

When experiencing burnout, a weekend off could likely assist reduce the sensation, however it's going to now not help you cast off it for specific.

To get over burnout for appropriate and reset your lifestyles, you want to begin residing a ultra-modern way of lifestyles. You need to make adjustments for your life and observe through with those changes.

Some of the subjects to help you get over burnout and reset are:

Sleep to Rest

Burnout consequences in a lack of sleep, worsening the state of affairs within the manner.

When experiencing burnout, you may war to doze off; you are in all likelihood to awaken a few times within the nighttime or awaken very early earlier than your alarm goes off. As a result, you begin your day tired.

A lack of sufficient sleep reduces your productivity and attention, and at the quit of the day, you locate yourself experiencing extra burnout because of the diverse obligations you may't appear to finish in time. When night time time comes, thoughts preserve you up, and the cycle continues, on and on, on a loop.

To get over burnout, you need to learn how to sleep to relaxation for at least 7 hours every night time. Getting sufficient sleep will assist you loosen up and repair your strength, providing you with "a easy head" every morning.

You turns into more centered, discover it easy to treatment problems, and most importantly, you may manipulate to preserve up along aspect your time table and duties. That method you can not experience most symptoms related to burnout, e.G., tension, demanding, lack of motivation, or strain.

Also, thinking about that loss of sleep consequences in impulsive, emotional behaviors, e.G., without issue becoming irritable, unhappy, or indignant, getting enough sleep will assist beautify your feelings and temper consequently lowering burnout.

Below are a number of the subjects you can do to enhance your sleep:

#: Have a bedtime ordinary

Do you have "sleep" on your every day time table in which you have got set aside 7 hours for sleep? If now not, you need to do that right away. Train your body to adapt to a snooze-wake cycle with the aid of drowsing and waking up at the same time every day.

For instance, in case you visit mattress at 8 PM and awaken at 5 AM, make this your ordinary routine. If you convert your habitual at some stage inside the weekends or off days, limit it to an hour's difference so that you do now not intervene collectively at the side of your cycle.

When it's bedtime, however you can't doze off inner 20-half-hour, get away from mattress and have a look at a ebook, take note of gentle song, or perform a little detail interesting. Since you're psychologically

31

organized to sleep, you can with out trouble get bored with some thing you pick out to do and find out it clean to go along with the drift off to sleep as fast as you get decrease lower back to mattress.

#: Limit your naps

To enhance your sleep, avoid taking extended naps in the direction of the day, i.E., make certain you do now not nap for more than half-hour. However, this does not endorse you could take numerous half of-hour naps in an afternoon; you can, but if you surely have to relaxation ultimately of the day, one 30-mins nap is sufficient.

Also, avoid drowsing too overdue in the night time, as this will have an effect for your sleep-wake cycle. However, if you paintings night shifts, you will want to take an middle of the night nap (an hour or earlier than artwork) to assist lessen sleep debt and enhance your alertness and consciousness.

#: Clear your mind

If you have got worries or issues approximately something earlier than going to mattress, you want to smooth them. Have a quick meditation and rest exercising with the useful aid of following those simple steps:

•Lie on your another time for your mattress and lightly close to your eyes.

•Take some breaths inside and outside, noticing how your chest rises and falls.

•Bring your attention in your respiratory pattern and slowly shift it on your thoughts.

•Notice all of the thoughts as they come and skip, with out judging or suppressing; handiest have a examine.

•Stay in this function for spherical 5 mins

•Slowly carry your attention again for your breathing

•Open your eyes when prepared.

You will go to sleep less tough after this exercise.

If this exercising doesn't work, write down steady thoughts which could't seem to go away. If the bothersome idea is ready a few issue you could take care of at that aspect, then do it, e.G., putting your alarm, taking your remedy, or checking if your baby is tucked in. If it's far some component you can not address proper then, e.G., a meeting with a client day after today, promise your self to study it in the morning.

#: Take a heat bathtub

Taking a warm tub 2 hours in advance than your bedtime will help loosen up your muscle corporations, making it clean to nod off. Sometimes, you can boom the exciting impact via along with chamomile in your bathtub/bathe water, i.E., located 2 spoons of chamomile in a bowl of boiling water.

Stir, depart it for 10 mins, then sieve as you pour it into the bath.

Also, you can diffuse lavender oil in your mattress room or placed a lavender bag below your pillow because lavender has a relaxing and exciting impact.

#: Watch what you eat or drink

A hungry belly would possibly likely wake you up inside the nighttime, on the identical time as a crammed belly might supply pain this is probably to keep you up.

Avoid huge or heavy food for supper, e.G., proteins, and commonly take your meal as a minimum 2 hours in advance than bedtime to offer your frame time to digest maximum of the food.

If you be   with the useful resource of "stressed legs" at the same time as dozing, include more magnesium on your night time meals, e.G., dried figs, nuts, seeds, rye bread, kale, and broccoli. Magnesium permits calm and loosen up the nerves and the muscular tissues.

Avoid caffeine and nicotine 4-6 hours earlier than sleep time because of the reality their stimulating consequences take time to put on off, which can have an impact for your napping cycle. Also, avoid alcoholic liquids. Yes, alcohol may additionally additionally depart you feeling sleepy, but it would wake you up inside the middle of the night.

You also can use a few natural teas regarded for his or her ability to prompt or promote sleep. Such natural teas embody St. John's Wort, hawthorn berries, lemon balm, inexperienced mint, hops, kava-kava, valerian, chamomile plant life, and passionflowers.

#: Make your bed room a "restful surroundings"

Bright mild inside the nighttime or the morning can disenchanted your biological clock. Hence, spend money on precise curtains or some room-darkening solar shades to lessen the moderate.

Too a good buy bloodless or an excessive amount of warm temperature impacts your sleep pattern at night time. Depending on the area, use a fan or an AC (air-conditioner) to modify the temperatures for your mattress room.

Make top notch the environment is quiet thru switching off any noise source in your property. If the noise is from topics or situations you cannot manipulate, e.G., low flying plane or the buddies, bear in mind the use of earplugs.

The above guidelines will assist you sleep to relaxation; exercising them every night.

NOTE: Unless prescribed via using a health practitioner, avoid using snoozing capsules due to the truth taking slumbering drugs, mainly regularly, will have an impact for your respiratory organs. Also, dozing drugs are addictive, and at the same time as you keep in mind that their "sleep impact" is not herbal, you are likely to evoke with a hangover or feeling worn-out each day as opposed to snug and refreshed.

Exercise

A take a look at published in the magazine "Physiology and Behaviour" says that researchers tasked ninety nine healthy people with inducing intellectual exhaustion via engaging in a 60 minutes cognitive check. The researcher cut up the have a have a study individuals into three organizations.

One business organization watched a 30 minutes movie; the subsequent organization engaged in moderate exercising on a treadmill for half-hour, whilst the final agency engaged in easy stretching bodily video games for 1/2-hour.

The researchers then assessed all of the human beings for tiredness, temper, motivation, cognitive flexibility, and restlessness. They determined that the human beings in the companies that exercised had a better and faster recovery approach from all the above states than folks who did no longer. Based on this test, we can cease that to recover from burnout, you need to embody workout on your time table.

Exercise helps lessen fatigue, improves cognitive characteristic, reduces emotional exhaustion, decreases mental pressure, and improves highbrow health and familiar well-being. Every day, set apart half-hour for exercise. Do some aspect is on hand and powerful for you, i.E., you can sign on for fitness center sessions or exercise from domestic —some thing works for you.

Yes, you already enjoy worn out and in all likelihood thinking how you may make it thru exercising intervals each day.

Here are a few pointers to help you:

#: Get commenced out out

You probable don't have the incentive, but actually positioned in your exercising clothes and get began out. Walk to the gym or strive diverse heat-up bodily games like taking walks in area or squats. These sports activities activities reason the producing of epinephrine and norepinephrine, hormones that act right now to energise you at some stage in the periods.

#: Do no longer be too difficult on your self

You don't must do extreme sporting sports to prevent burnout. Hence, do now not perform an workout that makes you enjoy uncomfortable or one you cannot do quite actually. Pushing yourself too rapid or too tough is probably to go away you fatigued— in preference to relieving it.

According to a observe completed through the University of Georgia, low-intensity bodily sports offer short and lengthy-term results at reducing burnout. So, besides you experience organized for immoderate-intensity wearing sports, do now not pressure or stress your self.

Some of the low-depth carrying sports you could attempt are:

•Cardiovascular sports activities: They substantially have an impact on the producing of endorphins a good way to leave you feeling correct. Also, at some point of cardiovascular physical activities, your thoughts will connect to your movement. That manner you can forget about your irritations and strain and enjoy body and thoughts relaxation. Some cardiovascular physical video games you could attempt are going for walks, swimming, boxing, dancing, jumping rope, prepared sports activities activities, cycling, trekking, rowing, brisk strolling, hula-hooping, and jogging in vicinity.

•Yoga, Pilates, and Tai Chi: These sporting sports activities will help you popularity on stretching and breathing while being aware,

thereby boosting your energy and mood —
related to burnout. Yes, you want time to
learn how to stability fatigue and power,
and along side one yoga, Pilates, or Tai Chi
consultation in line with week for your
workout normal will assist you get there.

#: Exercise outdoor

Occasionally, take your exercising out of
doors because of the truth exercise out of
doors will help you enjoy extra revitalized,
experience a large discount of despair,
pressure, anxiety, and confusion, and
substantially enhance your strength tiers.

#: Exercise often

To make it via your recovery adventure, you
need to be ordinary in your exercising
everyday. If it sluggish desk says, "Exercise,"
do not discover excuses to bypass your
session. Yes, a few unavoidable situations
could likely occur, however discover a way
to squeeze for your half-hour exercise
consultation. You should live stoically

devoted for this plan to achieve success. If you may, have a exercise accomplice who will assist keep you at the proper music and induced every time you experience like having a "cheat day."

NOTE: Schedule your workout inside the morning or within the course of the day or at least 1-2 hours in advance than bedtime to guard your sleep cycle. Yes, workout enables loosen up the frame and mind, thereby enhancing your slumbering behavior, but on the equal time as you do it proper in advance than going to mattress, the exertion from walking out ought to likely preserve you enormous-aware.

Chapter 4: Adopt A Healthy Diet

What you consume every day can be very important because it determines your strength tiers. For example, in case you bypass food most of the time, your blood sugar degrees will maintain losing, major to low electricity levels and mood, worsening burnout.

To save you this, begin having nutritious food and healthy snacks. The primary styles of food to include in your every day weight-reduction plan are:

#: Complex carbohydrates

Carbohydrates are famous for their capability to help the thoughts produce serotonin (feel-precise chemical materials). Hence, making them your pal is a remarkable idea.

An even higher concept is choosing complex carbohydrates over easy carbohydrates because complex carbohydrates are sluggish to digest. That manner they'll now not motive blood sugar spikes which can leave you feeling energized one minute and espresso on power the next—complex carbohydrates provide a stable electricity deliver.

Some complicated carbohydrates you may encompass on your weight loss plan are complete grains like brown rice, barley, quinoa, oats, and whole wheat. Some easy carbohydrates to avoid are sugary beverages and juices, breakfast cereals, fruit juice pay attention, and baked goods with added sugar.

#: Healthy fats

Including food with healthy fats and omega 3s on your eating regimen is important.

Research has proven that they help lessen and prevent depression, assist combat fatigue through sharpening and optimizing your thoughts, assist sell sleep and keep healthful blood sugar tiers, thereby boosting your temper, energy, and motivation.

Fish, specially tuna, salmon, sardines, herring, anchovies, trout, and mackerel, are the amazing assets of healthful fats and omega 3s.

If you're a vegetarian, soy merchandise, nuts (mainly walnuts), rapeseed, hemp seed, linseed, and pumpkin seeds are your great guess for wholesome fats.

#: High fiber veggies and give up end result

Research shows that fiber-wealthy food permits relieve tension and pressure (the number one reasons of burnout) due to the fact fiber facilitates protect the intestine, which produces ninety% of the hormone serotonin (satisfied hormone).

Additionally, nutrients discovered in fiber assist feed and shield probiotics (beneficial micro organism inside the gut) that can have an impact on thoughts function. For example, an inflamed gut negatively affects mind function (through the vagus nerve), inflicting tension, stress, reminiscence loss, and depression.

Therefore, make certain all your food comprise cease end result and vegetables because they are specific assets of fiber. Examples of culmination with immoderate degrees of fiber are strawberries (2%), pears (3.1%), broccoli (2.6%), and carrots (2.Eight%).

#: A glass of milk in advance than bed

Yes, a glass of milk is good for unwinding and falling asleep. Milk is a whole food with proteins, carbohydrates, fats, minerals, and nutrients and may be a notable beautify on your recuperation adventure. Milk has immoderate ranges of tryptophan that assist the body produce serotonin, a hormone recognised for its capacity to lessen tension. Also, milk is wealthy in melatonin, whose most vital function is to modify the sleep-wake cycle.

That technique eating a tumbler of milk earlier than bedtime will help growth the stages of the hormone melatonin, signaling your body to get equipped to fall asleep. In addition, the immoderate tiers of calcium in milk assist ease mood swings, fatigue, or highbrow and physical exhaustion.

Include a tumbler of milk in your night time time habitual to assist reduce burnout and assist your self go to sleep less complicated.

#: Protein

Whether plant or animal-based honestly, proteins assist maintain balanced blood sugar ranges, which, in flip, help stabilize your electricity and temper levels.

#: Magnesium

Magnesium enables with muscle relaxation, electricity manufacturing, and safety of the apprehensive tool —elements which is probably affected at some point of burnout. Some belongings of magnesium are almonds, seeds, quinoa, kidney beans, and inexperienced greens. If you do not take maximum of these foods, you may have magnesium citrate nutritional dietary supplements.

In addition, extraordinary stuff you have to hold in hobby with reference to adopting a wholesome weight loss plan are:

• Limit the quantity of alcohol you eat to 4-five glasses every week because of the truth alcohol can cause advanced paranoia, tension, and hangovers, major to extra pressure and burnout. Also, excessive alcohol consumption can result in dependence or even dependancy.

• If you smoke, begin by using the use of getting "smoke-free" days (possibly three days in line with week) and paintings inside the path of sincerely stopping this habit. Look for the extremely good manner to give up smoking. Studies display that people who smoke experience appreciably more melancholy and fatigue degrees than non-those who smoke.

• Start via searching for to stop eating espresso or reduce your espresso consumption. You can start sluggish, like going a day or two without coffee, then boom the length until you may skip numerous days or possibly weeks without espresso. Drinking a cup of espresso could make you experience more alert because it promotes the manufacturing of extra adrenaline, but even as it wears off, it leaves you feeling mentally and physical exhausted.

• Try food you haven't had earlier than. Make your food thrilling and interesting with the aid of trying a brand new dish or recipe each week to make sure you constantly have something to sit up for — meal-practical.

• Avoid having paintings breakfast or lunch. Take your breakfast at domestic each day earlier than going to art work, and constantly located your artwork aside in the direction of lunch breaks. When you are not stressing about art work, you can revel in your food, and your digestion will get going well. You will no longer ought to spend your days with a bloated belly or feeling tired after meals.

If you're experiencing stomach complications as a result of burnout:

• Regularly have smoothies, soups, and heat liquids. For example, upload 1 part of cabbage juice with 2 components of carrot juice, drink turmeric tea, cashew-lime smoothie, or turmeric milk. Drinking any of those will provide you with a warm temperature and comforting feeling that allows you to purpose rest.

• After a meal, drink a cup of mint tea if viable. Also, ensure to drink at least 8 glasses of water every day. The human frame is 60% water—in all body organs and cells. This water contains minerals and salts needed inside the frame for diverse capabilities. When you do now not drink enough water, you switch out to be dehydrated. Dehydration disrupts frame strategies, and you start to revel in complications and fatigue. Also, for the purpose that thoughts doesn't feature properly without sufficient water, it turns into gradual at sending neurological signals, fundamental to intellectual exhaustion, interest disturbing situations, and a slow temper. To save you maximum of those and lots of more outcomes of dehydration from occurring, drink as plenty water as feasible.

• Regularly drink aloe Vera juice because it enables restore the belly's mucous membrane. You will need approximately 99% pure Aloe Vera juice, and to make it drinkable, dilute it with as plenty water as feasible.

Strive to Have Better Work-Life Balance

If you're experiencing burnout that leaves you taking walks all of the time, you want to recognize one thing: as an grownup, juggling amongst paintings and personal existence will commonly be a assignment.

Fortunately, you could create a balance amongst your artwork and personal lifestyles with the resource of following the ones suggestions:

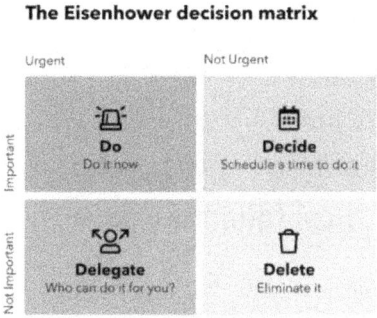

The Eisenhower decision matrix

	Urgent	Not Urgent
Important	**Do** Do it now	**Decide** Schedule a time to do it
Not Important	**Delegate** Who can do it for you?	**Delete** Eliminate it

#: Learn how to say "No"

You want to learn how to located obstacles amongst your paintings and personal existence. Not the whole lot at work is yours to attend to, and now not everything is pressing.

To studies while to say "No" at artwork, use the Eisenhower Matrix with the intention to help distinguish a number of the vital and pressing duties to avoid falling into the "Urgency lure."

In your magazine or computer, create a 2×2 matrix and label the 4 quadrants as showed within the diagram above, i.E., urgent and important (quadrant 1), essential and not pressing (quadrant 2) pressing but not crucial (quadrant three), and not pressing and not critical (quadrant four).

Quadrant 1

In the urgent and critical quadrant, only have the inevitable obligations that require your instant hobby. For instance, closing-minute cut-off dates, protecting for your colleague or employee who referred to as in ill, or a patron with a pressing rely.

Usually, those responsibilities have brief-term goals, and even as a assignment lies in this magnificence, you want to do it as short as viable. Avoid any distractions whilst operating on those obligations and responsibilities genuinely so they do not absorb the time committed to great responsibilities.

Quadrant 2

In the essential and not urgent quadrant, usually have the duties that don't have remaining dates but are vital and essential to attaining your long-term goals.

These are the responsibilities you may eliminate for a while and cope with the responsibilities in quadrant 1. Examples of those responsibilities and duties are mastering a contemporary talent, retaining up with modern career developments, planning for projects, exercising, and networking.

For the responsibilities in this phase, agenda the exceptional time to do them. Ensure you attend to them with the outstanding plan and approach because those responsibilities determine if you can have many obligations in quadrant one.

For example, if you fail to devise in your prolonged-time period responsibilities, you will likely find your self with urgent and important responsibilities. That way you may be setting aside your lengthy-time period obligations more than regularly than no longer, and on the prevent of the day, you discover your self overwhelmed, feeling stuck, and experiencing extra burnout.

In this quadrant, you may be focusing on opportunities and growth. Hence, at the same time as you succeed in any mission right right here, you could see progress on your artwork and life, if you need to move away you feeling endorsed.

If you advocate and attention on the essential however not pressing obligations and responsibilities, you may be growing more time on your personal lifestyles due to the reality many critical duties will now not enter quadrant 1. Hence, you'll now not need to alternate some time table for obligations you could have done earlier.

Quadrant three

In the pressing however not essential quadrant, region the duties that do not take you in the direction of dreams however come from specific humans's expectancies of you. Most of the responsibilities in this quadrant are pressing but primarily based on a person else's priorities and obligations.

For instance, a co-employee ought to in all likelihood interrupt you more than as speedy as to inform you approximately their new dreams, or a colleague may also ask you to represent him in a meeting due to the truth he has to do something else, or you will likely enjoy the want to answer to texts or emails each time your smartphone notifies you of the same.

When in any situation, ask your self how its urgency contributes in your short-time period or prolonged-term goals. When the challenge is some element you may automate or delegate, don't hesitate to perform that.

For instance, can your children do the dishes? Ask them to do so. Can your employee go to a exceptional assembly and take notes for you? Send him/her. Can you get a shop that gives you products in preference to picking them up from the store in my view? Make the order.

If you can't automate or delegate a undertaking, then look for a direct answer however do not permit it distract you out of some time table. For example, however the reality which you cannot delegate your smartphone, you could flip off notifications at the same time as strolling. You can not delegate an emergency project given to you with the aid of your supervisor to a co-employee, but you could negotiate your workload together together with your boss. If a person genuinely dreams your help, you may be easy on how lots time you may spare, and any request from the character past the said time want to accumulate a genuine "no."

Quadrant four

The last listing of responsibilities need to be those subjects that aren't pressing and now not vital. These duties do now not make contributions some issue worthwhile to your plans, goals, or duties however frequently soak up a whole lot time. They are why you procrastinate, simplest to experience beaten while the essential duties get to quadrant 1.

Such duties embody immoderate on-line browsing, spending hours looking TV, gossiping at the side of your colleagues, mindlessly scrolling via your cellular cellphone, or immoderate purchasing.

You need to drop the tasks in this quadrant because they absorb a while and leave you with unaccomplished obligations and desires. Learn how to mention "No" to those duties; it will help you create time for your personal life.

Before figuring out a way to method any given situation at artwork or possibly at home, check the state of affairs and vicinity it in the right quadrant to assist yourself create stability in existence.

#: Take breaks

It is probably tough to take breaks while at artwork because of the fact the truth is that you could't surely go away your station for five-10 mins every 2-3 hours with the useful resource of way of telling your supervisor, "I am taking a smash." However, you could take breaks while despite the fact that at your table; 30 seconds to 1 minute is all you need.

Here are a number of the stretches you can

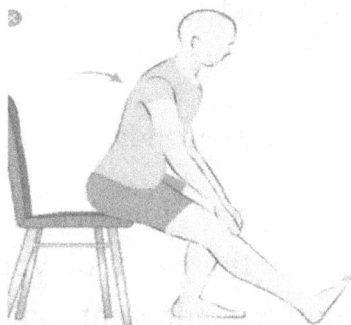

attempt at the equal time as at paintings:

Chapter 5: Hamstring Stretch

•While seated, make bigger your proper leg outward and maintain your left foot flat on the ground with its knee at ninety ranges.

•Reach beforehand such that your fingertips are on your right toes.

•Hold for 20 to 30 seconds.

•Return to starting function and switch aspects, i.E., at the facet of your left leg prolonged outward and right foot flat at the floor.

•Try this stretch with each legs prolonged outward.

Shoulder shrug

•While for your chair, sit down down along with your once more without delay and feet flat at the floor.

•With your arms in your lap or putting on your components, decorate your shoulders.

•Drop them.

•Repeat for 1o to 15 instances.

Overhead element gain

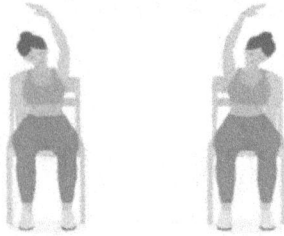

•While for your chair, sit down down along with your returned at once and feet flat on the ground.

•Extend one arm overhead and permit the opposite hold to your aspects.

•Reach to the alternative element collectively along with your extended arm.

•Hold for 20- 30 seconds.

•Switch fingers.

When you do stretches as frequently as possible and take all the breaks given through your boss, you may beautify your concentration, feel engaged on your work, lessen stress, and make your artwork extra interesting, thereby reducing burnout.

If you make money working from home, you want to create a piece-life balance. Most those who make money working from home will be predisposed to paintings all the time, which consist of the weekends or past due nights, which leads to imbalances amongst their artwork and personal lifestyles.

To ensure you create this stability as you earn a living from home:

•Have a routine

Just as humans running in places of work have a morning recurring, you want to have one. Don't simply wake up and get right to artwork. When you awaken, have a cup of tea, shower, meditate, check a few pages of your contemporary novel, get a newspaper and undergo it. Having a morning regular will mentally and physical prepare you for the day's activities, increasing your productiveness.

Also, have a ordinary or time table such as all of the activities or belongings you need to perform every day. Yes, you are up and prepared, however what next? Try distinct exercises to make your lifestyles interesting.

For instance, you could have a schedule in that you decide for four non-prevent days regular with week or 4 separate days of each week. Make superb to agenda for work when you are best.

Some human beings are maximum alert inside the morning, a few within the afternoon, whilst others decide on running within the nighttime. Use your most effective time to create and observe a bit ordinary that permits you create a balanced life that works to help you lessen and save you burnout.

In some time table, encompass round 5 mins breaks after each forty five minutes. During the ones five minutes, take a stroll across the out of doors lawn, do some stretches, have a snack, or drink a few warm beverage. Doing this may permit your thoughts and frame to loosen up; resultantly, you'll manipulate to cowl hundreds with out experiencing exhaustion or fatigue.

• Avoid distraction

Distractions lower your productiveness and leave you feeling like you have were given been running at the identical project for hundreds of years. They soak up it slow, forcing you to use the time you scheduled for your non-public life to finish your responsibilities. At day's cease, you may discover yourself with unattended responsibilities or responsibilities, with a purpose to boom your stress and anxiety levels.

Avoid this via letting your own family realize that they should no longer come into your place of business even as you're strolling until it's an emergency. Stay far out of your mobile phone, social media payments, or TV at some point of operating hours.

Also, your computing device must not be for your dwelling areas like your mattress room or living room as you're in all likelihood to be distracted. Instead, installation your place of work in the room with the least website online site visitors inside the house.

•Know at the same time as to prevent

It might be tempting to finish a project or prep for your subsequent mission after your scheduled work hours are up. Do your fine to keep away from that.

If you are out for the weekend, do now not supply your art work with you. Do no longer test your emails for a mission or patron's updates if it's far your sleep time. This tendency to show every time to artwork time can create paintings-private lifestyles imbalance and reason fatigue and burnout. Therefore, even as fantastic artwork is not at the time table, do not do it except it is urgent and vital —the primary quadrant.

Practice Positive Thinking

In addition to looking after your self and converting your manner of existence, you need to learn how to prevent awful mind due to the fact they play a big feature in number one to burnout.

Understand that you could face traumatic situations, experience strain, fail, make mistakes, and revel in setbacks; it's an inevitable part of lifestyles. How you recognize those conditions will determine in case you recover from burnout or fall deeper into the cycle.

For instance, if you preserve telling yourself you are not appropriate enough to live in a relationship or you may in no manner reach your business organisation, even after converting your life-style, those poor mind will result in pressure. And, due to the fact you do not recognize a way to deal with such mind in reality, you will discover your self stuck in burnout.

Fortunately, researchers have demonstrated that operating closer to great wondering allows control stress, lowers despair, boosts temper, improves bodily and mental well-being, effects in better resistance to illnesses, and masses of various health advantages.

Let us take a look at steps you could take to expand a powerful mind-set:

#: Maintain a gratitude mag

When you continuously popularity on what you do not have or what is inaccurate for your existence, it fills your thoughts with terrible thoughts, making it tough to do anything or perhaps make any adjustments.

On the other hand, even as you begin thinking about all the property you are thankful for, your thoughts moves proper into a great state wherein you begin thinking about although first rate things aren't going well, various things are doing quite well, and that is the first-rate mind-set to get transferring and exchange. Therefore, it's miles important to begin operating closer to gratitude.

Get your self a gratitude magazine and undertake the every day addiction of writing a few issue in it, irrespective of how small it's far. It likely sounds tacky, however while you create time to mirror at the belongings you are thankful for, you can start paying more interest to the fine factors of your existence.

For instance, write down such things as, "I finished my task in time," "I am healthful," "I have a supportive companion or pal," "I closed a deal nowadays," or "I clearly have a stunning family."

Expressing gratefulness for the notable matters for your existence gives more pleasure and which means that to your lifestyles, leaving no room for bad thoughts.

#: Embrace your successes

Your wins are yours to recognize, encompass, appreciate, and have amusing. Stop downplaying your achievements through manner of announcing, "Anyone ought to do what I did" or, "I really were given fortunate." Even although every body ought to have finished it, you are the only who did it due to the fact you install some attempt. Even in situations in that you did not prevail, it is important to recognize that you tried because it's best sincere to comprehend your efforts.

Giving yourself credit for your efforts and successes will make you experience glad and preferred. You will become stimulated and start longing for more wins, on the way to help you make bigger a extra quality outlook in your existence.

Also, while desired or celebrated through others, take delight within the ones moments. For example, if your patron thank you you for great services or, when your boss recognizes your difficult artwork, do now not take it as a right. Instead, word the pleasure such moments provide you with (small or huge) and allow yourself enjoy the first-rate emotions or thoughts. When you're making it your addiction to revel in the fine instances, you boom streams of high awesome feelings and thoughts that eventually turn out to be part of you.

#: Experience terrible concept while need be

Yes, nice thoughts will assist you lessen pressure and recover from burnout however preserve in mind that not all situations call for great responses. For instance, in case you lose your biggest customer, express your poor emotions and mind about the scenario to your family or buddies. It will help you speak the need for their aid (financially or emotionally). Or, letting your self get indignant while handled unfairly at work can inspire you to take the vital moves, e.G., rise up for your self.

When experiencing negative feelings, do no longer truly push them apart because of the fact this could sooner or later purpose negative results. Instead, emerge as aware of their beginning vicinity and search for the nice manner to address them.

#: Practice excellent self-communicate

Make it a rule now not to inform yourself a few component you wouldn't say to someone else. Instead, constantly be gentle and kind to yourself. Anytime a terrible idea crosses your mind, understand it and replace it with a excellent one.

For instance, in case your assignment is hard, as opposed to pronouncing to yourself, "It is really too complex for me," say, "Let me technique it from a one-of-a-kind angle." Or, if you discover your self handling a contemporary mission, do now not say, "I in truth have in no way finished this earlier than. I don't anticipate I may be powerful at it." Instead, remind your self that it is a cutting-edge opportunity to take a look at and growth.

Remember that you could fail or gather any scenario. However, you could never apprehend the fact if you keep letting your negative thoughts convince you which you are not unique sufficient, which you are lazy, that you may in no way get better, or that exchange isn't always your detail. Doing so way you're deciding on to be a failure. Give yourself a chance by using looking beforehand to the extremely good in each situation and in case you fail, use that possibility to look at and put together for the subsequent time.

#: Surround your self with people with high remarkable mindsets

The humans round you substantially effect your mentality. If your friends need to complain, doubt themselves or others, and criticize the whole lot, you will most probably encompass their mindsets. That is why you want greater optimistic people to your life.

Spend greater time with folks who inspire you to do higher, those who accept as true with in themselves—and also you—humans you could visit for useful comments and recommendation, and people who aren't fearful of taking possibilities. Surround yourself with characteristic energy, and interior no time, you may additionally grow to be a excessive nice philosopher.

However, irrespective of who you surround yourself with, do no longer diploma yourself in competition to everyone. Yes, a few humans are doing higher than you, and others have higher capabilities. However, comparing your self to them will go away you doubting your self. You will extend more awful thoughts and emotions about your self, as a way to top notch go away you confused.

Learn How to Manage Stress after Recovering from Burnout

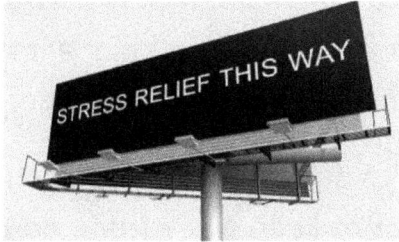

The above sections have pointers that have helped you apprehend and get over burnout, but what now? Although you need to hold running in the direction of all the referred to steps to save you burnout from reoccurring, you furthermore mght must discover ways to manipulate pressure.

Here are some recommendations which could assist up manage it:

Chapter 6: Identify Your Stress Triggers

Self-knowledge may be very powerful. When you understand what triggers your strain, you may understand a manner to quality approach the ones conditions.

If it's miles something or a person you can dispose of or keep away from, do it, e.G., a chum, a coursemate, or stress from social media. However, if it's miles some thing or a person you can't avoid, e.G., your boss, a project presentation, or your consumer, mentally put together for the upcoming pressure. Being prepared for stress will assist method or cope with the man or woman or state of affairs better and in a organized way.

For example, if you understand your colleagues reason your stress, rehearse a way to react or reply at the same time as you encounter each special. Create a highbrow image of the way you may act to help your self efficiently conquer pressure.

If you do not recognize your pressure triggers, usually have a diary. Then, every time you revel in stress, write down the nice state of affairs, the involved events, and the feelings and feelings related to the state of affairs. Keep doing this each time you enjoy forced; after a while, you could take a look at a sample on what or who triggers your stress.

Don't Be Hard On Yourself

Accept that no man or woman is right, and irrespective of how tough you attempt, you could make errors or fail. Stop stressing your self because of the reality you want perfection. Instead, do your first rate in every undertaking, obligation, or mission, take transport of the effects and recall to offer yourself the credit score you deserve.

Also, stop traumatic about matters beyond your control. Yes, you'll spend masses time stressing and traumatic approximately a scenario or a scenario, however this received't alternate the reality that there can be not something you could do. For instance, you can't change the beyond. Therefore, whether you want how subjects have become out or not, spending hours or days wondering and beating your self up for it won't make matters better. However, it is to your capacity to recognition on making your nowadays and day after today better than your the day past.

Open Up

When a few aspect is bothering you, do not in reality hold it to your self because it will consume you from inner. Instead, communicate to a person you receive as actual with with your emotions and emotions. Sharing lets in elevate the weight off your, thereby reducing pressure and clearing your thoughts, permitting you to approach the situation from a smooth thing of view.

Also, on the identical time as you open up, you may gather recommendation or possibly help —if viable— to help you deal with your scenario. Therefore, at the same time as you percentage your trouble or situation with a person else, and the individual offers to help, take it and take into account to unique your gratitude.

Develop a Sense of Humor

Do now not be too crucial all the time. When some thing is humorous, snort. Look for a few stand-up comedies, watch humorous clips on social media, and chortle at your buddies', colleagues,' or siblings' jokes. Laughing and being lighthearted allows you to lighten up and allows you experience better, even within the course of stressful times.

Also, chuckle at your self sometimes to help lighten your temper and decrease stress. It is ok to mirror in your lifestyles and snicker at a few funny reviews (even the demanding ones), so long as you do no longer harm your conceitedness or located yourself down.

Create Time for Hobbies

Doing a few factor you like or enjoy is a superb way of enjoyable your mind and decreasing stress. Therefore, each day, set aside 15 to half-hour for your pastimes, e.G., studying, gambling sports activities, writing, drawing, cooking, knitting, looking a film, gambling board video video games or gambling gambling cards, doing puzzles, or playing golfing. On days while you're experiencing strain, strive a contemporary hobby you would really like to research.

Your mind will prevent traumatic approximately the scenario inflicting you pressure and as an alternative popularity on studying the modern day know-how. Also, the pride and rush feeling of experiencing a few aspect for the primary time will depart you happy and relaxed.

Chapter 7: Find Different Ways To Relax , And To Relieve Tension

Identify Stressors by Keeping a Stress Diary

The process of identifying stressors may be more complicated than you believe. There are many things that can cause stress simultaneously but some things are more difficult than others. It could be that your procrastination or lack of organization is the cause of the stress and not you work or the task you're conducting work on.

Try to keep a daily diary of your stress for about a week to track the stresses that you face in your everyday life. By using the example in the table, you can write down the details below. You can examine this information in order to pinpoint the root of your anxiety. If you're fortunate enough to have a trustworthy family member or partner, invite them to read through your journals together with you.

If you're stressed (date/time)

What is the reason for the stress (if you know the source)

What did you do to deal with the stressors and

How did you reduce stress?

Find Ways to Avoid Stressors

Change Any Situation You Can

Be aware of traffic and avoid it by using the public transportation system or joining a carpool for an enjoyable conversation an enjoyable diverting activity.

Be aware of how much time you are spending on people who stress you.

You should have plenty of time to do some errands, or even get your project completed. Make sure to set your clock and watch in the forward position by five or 10 minutes, so you're in time.

Shut off all technology especially prior to going to bed to ensure that you don't have to worry about the quality of your sleep. It doesn't matter if it's TV or computer the absence of distraction allows you to concentrate on your work as well as makes you less vulnerable to the people around you who may increase stress levels.

Utilize a central wall or paper calendar for coordinating your family's activities and work. Think about color-coding the calendar for every person.

Schedule time in your day to do exercise and for relaxation and rest. Then don't cancel.

Make a list of your tasks that you can keep forever in a notebook, written on paper, your smartphone, or on your laptop. (There's even an Sticky Notes computer app so you can have the list handy on the desktop of your computer.) Every day, determine what items are essential to have, what you should get, and take them off. Then, move the rest towards the end of your list, or take them off in the event that you're able to.

Beware of distractions that can be general, such as the phone or email in the course of meeting deadlines or hang around with your family or friends.

Make time to organize your grocery shopping and/or meal plans during your week. Making a few preparations could save you time over the long term and save you shopping trips or a long, inefficient trip to the town.

Learn to Say No

Naturally, it's impossible to refuse to do every single thing. There are times when your job demands you to finish certain jobs in a certain amount of time. Therefore, you might not be able to refuse in front of your manager. You cannot turn down requests. Don't let yourself be influenced by reason to accept the burden you're not capable of handling. There is no one who knows better about your needs than you.

Don't forget that even if you're able to squeeze things into your daily schedule does not necessarily mean that you must. If you are taking on more tasks, it is necessary to give up something else crucial to you, like the much-needed time to relax.

If you've got the enough time, expertise or cash, you can tell your boss clearly and politely in the event that you are running out of items to do. Sometimes , it's best to provide an easy apology, "I am always willing to help, however I'm not in a position to do so currently. That's it.

If you are pressured by someone to give an explanation, just say to the fact that it doesn't match your agenda. The person is not obligated to provide further explanations.

If you're having trouble learning to assert yourself immediately you can consider rethinking your options and reach out to the person following a review of their calendar.

If you'd like to be there but aren't able to take on full responsibility you can say that I'm not responsible but I might be able to

_____.

Do not waste time guilt-ridden and make a list of your to-do list that you've already finished!

Change Your Approach or Attitude to Be More Positive

The research shows that positive attitudes can benefit your heart. However, nobody is happy or positive at all times. People feel anxious, sad at times, and even overwhelmed often. People who are happy and positive have a better chance of avoiding frustration and achieve a state of joy more easily in the event that life isn't able to accept them.

Getting Happier

Studies have shown that there are a variety of ways to boost your mood, which includes these:

Accept what you cannot modify and stop to be concerned about small issues. Make a list of things you can alter, including the way you think and approach your life.

Make a journal of gratitude in order to make it a point to identify at least one thing you're thankful for every day. It will help you maintain an optimistic outlook. The situation can become more severe.

Maintain positive relationships with people around you. Make it a priority to build relationships with your family and friends. They are the ones who give life meaning.

The support and love that your loved ones provide is not often seen.

Give a hand to help. Giving back to those that are in need will automatically increase feelings of appreciation.

Never hesitate asking for assistance. If you're feeling overwhelmed It's fine to ask relatives and friends who can assist you. They could not even notice because it's always nice to feel loved. In addition, it's easy to return the favor.

Make every effort to exercise regularly.

Being active can help you to remain confident in your thinking because it releases joy chemical (called endorphins).

Also, you will feel more comfortable whenever you're in better physically.

Get a Pet! The presence of a cat or dog that you can keep company with will reduce blood pressure. Additionally, caring for your pet can be a gratifying as well as physically demanding.

Take advantage of the wonders and joys that life has to offer. Be sure to keep your goals for the future on your mind, but strive to be present and not fret too much about the future.

What to do when you are angry?

Everyone is angry at least once in a while. However, anger can increase your risk of suffering from heart health. Therefore, if you cannot avoid getting annoyed in the first place It is best to manage it as calmly as quickly, clearly, and directly as is possible. Follow these suggestions:

Put your tongue out. Make a count of 10 to stop your anger from running prior to pondering your words.

Getaway if necessary. Let you let your anger recede and gain a better understanding of the issue. It will help you avoid making decisions or saying things are regrettable. It also aids in ease stress.

Let your emotions be known: Once you've calmed enough, you'll be more comfortable discussing your concerns with the person worried, instead of allowing it to get out of hand. If you find it helpful, think about recording your thoughts as a letter that you can give to the person, or you could write a letter in order to organize your thoughts. discard it in the next step, then talk directly with the individual. It is important to start the sentences with "I feel ... instead of you made me. Which can lead to the listener becoming be defensive.

Find the solution. Do not think about the things that made your angry. Focus on the things both of you will do to prevent this from happening again.

Refuse to forgive and tell them I am sorry. Studies show that forgiveness is able to aid the heart. It is believed that If you keep holding onto anger, angry feelings, resentment and hatred and stress, it can cause. Therefore, forgiveness is a great way to in healing your heart. Don't forget to forget about yourself!

Relax, smile even more and be careful to avoid repeating yourself! The most effective way to handle anger is to stay away from getting anger in the first place.

Learn New Ways to Relax and Relieve Stress

The way you feel stressed is different to everyone. Therefore, it is natural that there are numerous methods to relieve stress and relax. tension. It is a vicious cycle of stress that is tough to end. The best way to prevent being overwhelmed with stress is to routinely set aside some me time you can take each day.

It could take 10-minutes or even an hour; it's all up for the individual. It is possible to do the same thing each day, or shift the routine to a new one, based on how stressed out you feel. Choose what's best for your body. The key thing is to be aware of your stress levels and then take steps regularly to lower it.

Seeking Help

Do not be embarrassed to seek assistance in managing stress. Stress can cause a lot of stress even for those who are healthy. There are also medical issues like chronic depression or a general feeling of fatigue in relation to heart disease or operations on the heart. This can make getting through stressful times difficult or impossible. A licensed counselor psychotherapist, psychologist or psychiatrist will help you recognize and reduce stress within your daily life.

It is important to know that certain ailments like depression and anxiety might require medications to reduce anxiety. Your doctor can determine if you need medication.

Chapter 8: Acquaintances On Facebook

they'd like to get for Mother's Day, with the restriction that they could not offer me silly answers such as"Oh, I'd like the gift of a hand-made card and some spending time with my children. I was looking for honest and real responses.

The completely diverse responses were sweet, fun and inspiring. All mothers shared one thing They were looking to escape worry, stress, and anxiety. They wanted their husbands to stay at home and do their chores only for a day.

I was shocked. It's because I don't have a complete list of their husbands However, those I have met are strong, healthy and loving. They're great wives and fathers. What is the reason they all drop the ball? These mothers really need to take a break Many of them did not even consider it even possible. When we spoke, they as if perhaps someday they were sighing in awe. I felt their pain deeply within my bones.

There is no shortage of single mothers everyone is talking about the emotional stress (Mental Health) and the way it could affect single mothers.

In order to keep families in the water with modern parents, mothers have to remember an extensive list of tasks every day of the year including selling cakes for school and the quantity of toilet papers stored at the bottom of their basement. We are responsible for it that if we do not keep track of it, it will never be accomplished.

It's a challenge. It's exhausting to expend an enormous amount of mental energy to things, but especially like chaotic, busy and overwhelming as the process of starting the process of having a child, which I am aware of since I was once carrying the emotional weight of the family my on my own. It was physically exhausting as well as emotionally. I believed that I would never get rid of the burden.

Perhaps one day I would think. In the meantime, I was shattered with the weight of motherhood.

The third time my child arrived, I didn't have enough trouble remembering all the details, and certainly could not do everything. So I explored something a bit bizarre and even a bit scary. Husband. I was used to it as the taste of a hot potato. Then it became quite challenging. We're going to ask your patience for to me for a little.

It sounds easy It's not, however it was. The whole process began when I acknowledged one thing that was crucial: I was not able to handle all the burden on myself. If I had the chance however, I did not think that I needed to. We all were involved in this issue of family; why did the burden of my own mental health come on me?

After that, I realized the most important thing: I had a part of the blame in the amount of accountability I'd taken on. My husband had always wanted to be more involved, but was unsure of the best way to help; often I would not to assistance. He was unsure of what he wanted (because I believed that he must be able to) Sometimes he was just looking to control everything. I was used to controlling every aspect of my life and found it difficult to let my partner to conduct things in the way they were his preference.

That's why I took a bite in the two highs and asked for more help. It's also 365 days of the year, not only Mother's Day.

It was a matter of asking to get the proper type of assistance: instead of being an individual micromanager of the family, and randomly dispersing duties from right to left My husband was asked to take on certain duties by himself. Are you responsible for keeping track of this? Are you responsible for watching this? Do you have an appointment on your calendar on Wednesdays?

Engaging him in this manner allowed me to not have to think of asking for assistance I required (which just added to my anxiety) However, it was also a way for my husband to truly understand the dynamics of our relationship and step up to take on a crucial function. He didn't just check off boxes on the list of friends but he also didn't think about the person again. He became involved in the daily life in a way that he'd never been previously.

The outcome was amazing My husband was able to observe through his eyes what required to be completed He started with the tasks that were external, like chores around the house: when he went down to the basement unpacking the clothes into the hallway, cooking the salad to serve us after dinner, then take out the Cheerios beneath the table. In the end, his assistance moved to more internal matters like taking responsibility for all of the occupational therapy sessions for our son and instructed the kids to go and pick him up at any time they required some assistance (instead to interrupt me as I was at work) and offered the opportunity to attend teachers' conferences for parents during the lunch time so that they do not have to arrange childcare in the home.

He listened to our family's demands and the ways he could assist me, and I didn't need to seek his help. Children began to recognize him as an important source to help them solve their issues or satisfy the needs of their families. I felt my mental load shrink a little.

Three years later it is clear that there are issues I don't have to think about since they're part of our husband's burden rather than my own. He is aware that his house is getting a little crowded and is able to add it to his list of things to buy.

Discover what foods your child is allowed to eat as a snack on weekends or for lunch, and be proactive. The responsibility lies with the emergency items we carry in our home including flashlights and batteries to first aid kits as well as the bottled water.

At times, I will remind him of how valuable they can be, and that it's good to have some extra concerns to take care of. Much like most people who work in a team, he might not understand the task at hand, but he prefers to be particular about what he does. This shift also brought him benefits.

He's more comfortable when he is a wife and father. He is happy knowing that he's actually helping me. He did not hesitate when I told him I needed more time for me, and I can enjoy my time free of worry, guilt, or fear.

My Baby Never Stops Crying

Each time my child cry (a million times in a day!)

It's normal for babies to cry! It's important to possess the confidence of a professional film actor to ensure that this doesn't affect your. With a bit of time, you'll grow (or become closer) to this. It will be clear that your child will not be able to stop crying. And even if you are unable to react immediately,

Don't think your child's crying due to being unhappy or sad. It's very easy to experience. That's the reason we cry. Children do it to signal that they're exhausted, cold, wet and hungry. or just plain bored. If you're creating the foundation of a daily routine for your child, it is possible to typically tell when he is in need from the sounds of his tears. Is it possible that you are wrong, and at the end, are you incorrect?

She was at a secure location. It took her a few minutes to settle down. My son started screaming, and I talked for hours, screaming high-pitched in outbursts of screaming, and held my phone in order to be able to hear me experiencing. Then on Friday, I could not bear it any more, and I set her down in the crib, and then in the kitchen to see if we could work to get her back on track. In a matter of minutes! I realized the image of me, anxious and angry with him just added fuel to the flame. When I let him go, he was calm and peacefully. He kept quiet.

I am sometimes offended by my child

I am sure he's very sweet as a newborn. Yet, I often feel frustrated when I have to meet the needs of his breastfeeding throughout the day, frequently changing his diapers. Then I am guilt-ridden for this thought.

The first step is to take an exhale and realize that everyone feels exactly the same way, according to Patricia Hemby, a mother of two in Amarillo, Texas. True, many women feel that they only have to feel happiness and love to achieve this. And later, they are embarrassed in the event that they don't. This isn't the only hard job we're discussing.

The fact is that almost all mothers have a sense of responsibility [that they have to shoulder] to a certain level or the other.

It's also beneficial to view the whole picture, adds Kimberly Harrington of Burlington, Vermont mom of three.

Be sure to remind myself that difficult moments are only temporary, however also are the great times. I'd like to see the day come to an night is over as well as spitting and breastfeeding, I'm sure when they are it, the amazing things that come when you have a baby fragileness and love for the baby will disappear too.

I Am Not Sleeping Enough

I'm sick of not sleeping enough. It's difficult for me to go on time to nap in the middle of the day. How can I help?

Every book on infants as well as pediatricians appear to be saying exactly the same thing. Sleep as the baby rests. Oh sure. To other mothers who aren't, it's (hello!) It's time for a break and it's tough to find a moment of peace with that baby constantly needing attentiveness. When the sun is shining even when there are tears. If you're awake, it's fine, because there are plenty of different ways to sleep.

Jessica Darney Buhler of Elizabethtown, NY, mother of three-year-old Oakley extended her bedtime several hours, and discovered that it was effective for myself. I was stunned by how quickly my energy level increased, says the mother.

Tina Levinson from Burlington, Vermont requested her husband to take on during the day and play with her daughter Sadie to keep her entertained until she woke up at 6 am, he loved being with her. Levinson got two more time to be in silence.

In the case of Raab The reason I not rest, my husband and I share a bottle of milk in the evening. (If you're breastfeeding then you are able to express your milk, then pour it into bottles.) The most important thing to know about this method is that if your child awakes several timesthroughout the night, it is best to have Mom as well as Dad to be able to handle all the feedings. Then, are able to move on to the next night. in the event that he wakes up at 1AM and you miss 4 AM each of you will become exhausted. The best option is if both of you are sleeping continuously.

If you're planning to rest but are unable to sleep, switch off the alarm and make your bedroom as dark as is possible. The ear plugs also help to block out the sound that keeps your from getting sleepy. Also, don't stay asleep for too long. If you are sleeping for longer than one hour, you can fall into a slow-wake state. If you awake in this state, you'll feel less alert and uneasy than at the start. Keep your sleep time of 30-45 minutes each every day. It's enough to feel refreshed and rejuvenated.

I Want To Lose Weight

I want the body I have lost. But I'm too busy to make healthy choices and don't have the motivation to work out.

It's hard to tell how many times I've heard the same thing from moms who have just had babies. However, if you implement only a couple of small changes I can assure you that your weight loss will be rapid.

The first thing to do is not worry about an hour-long training session. Instead, divide it into 10 to 15 minute chunks throughout your days. The task will appear less daunting and more likely to keep going to it. Walk around or watch a great movie with your children while they sleep or perform strength training whilst having fun on your own. If you're at the gym, check out the babysitting service (at all gyms) or get your partner involved. Do some work for running or go swimming.

I blocked a few of my afternoon hours during the week from my working schedule and did not attend yoga classes, claims Stephanie Wegl. Because I am not able to access the class it is impossible to make an appointment, and am less likely to make a decision to cancel. The most difficult part is beginning. When you've finally done it you'll be surprised at how much energy you've got and how great you feel.

Are you looking to eat more healthily?

The key is planning ahead. Prepare a big portion of vegetable (the that you enjoy the most) and grill chicken breasts and roasts for the weekend to make amazing snacks during the week. Do not be stuck if do not have the best options.

The bag of dried fruit and nuts inside your bag for work, or put the apple and muesli in the food processor. Don't take a trip to the store without making certain that your children are provided with ready-made food. The same can be the case for yourself!

I Don't Trust My Instincts

Everybody says they believe in their gut instincts, however it's difficult to be sure in the beginning when you're not familiar with all this parenting squabbling.

As a newly parent, you're not sure of notion of what's going on, yet you're determined to do it the right way. In the process, I've observed many mothers leaving their thoughts to the experienced physician instead of listening to what they believe to be correct, however you do spend the most time with your child more than anybody else, and so you're a true professional.

Be sure to follow your instincts. Test what you believe works the best, and if you don't you can speed things up. Consult your doctor or your friends.

It's definitely an act of faith but it won't give you confidence in your motherhood when you don't accept the risk. As a baby My daughter, Freya, was always wanting to hold me all the time and was crying every time she left my arms. claims Tisha Crews Keller of Tallahassee, Florida. They will be spoilt but I am sure that I did what was right to Leah in order to ensure that she would be safe and feel loved.

She is finally out of this period. At 19 months, she's an self-reliant, pure, and definitely not a loving girl. It was a lot of faith to do my best to fulfill my mother's responsibility, but I'm so glad I was able to do it. Each time you achieve something like this, the greater you are convinced that you have faith you are a good mother , you will be able to make

Your instincts may be able to guide you. Nowadays, it's effortless to read the book, browse online, or contact relatives with questions regarding the child.

The fact that these suggestions are available is important, but you can reach a point that is overwhelming. I fell completely into the trap, and I read everything I could. That was the time I became anxious and I was most likely to question my choices.

The advice was numerous and advice, many of which was conflicting which made me less secure at the conclusion. I've established a rule of that I should continue to work until an extent and adhering to the things that feel comfortable.

Remember that the best of your judgments prove to be incorrect the result won't have devastating consequences for your child. Consider a different method. There's something to be said about how they can learn with each other. It's a big part of your relationship with your child. It also makes you more of a mother.

I'm looking for an interruption from nursing

Since my child is dependent that I also breastfeed. Additionally, I'm also the one who is scheduled as a maternity leaver. It would be great to have breaks from time to the time.

Then I told my husband that he'd need to stay at home the whole the day to play with our son. He did not have the burden of having going to work as his schedule was set and he only needed to look after himself. According to Kristy McCarthy Weight, a native of Annapolis, Maryland.

He then became adept with me reading, He could almost predict the times he would need time with me. In times when I felt tired My husband would suggest that NANA (his mother) visit our home. If I was tired I was exhausted, he'd suggest that I chauffeur our son around while I worked on my manicure. Do not feel guilty. have earned it, and you'll be a better parent because of this.

My House Is A Mess

My house is as if a baby bomb been exploded. It's a mess. It's been a while since I've had one second to get it cleaned up.

The most common solution among mothers who I talked towas to hire someone to take care of your home. I was not happy spending money however, it was worth it with regard to my emotional health and stress. The program doesn't need to be an annual offer (every 2 weeks will do) as well as it doesn't have to be expensive. Think of it not as an expense, rather as an investment for your child's education because period you'd to spend cleaning or dusting can now be yours.

If it's not feasible to get a professional to help, begin slowly. I washed each time my son went to take the time to nap for 15 minutes according to Pamela stone of Carlisle, Pennsylvania mother of Xavier 11, who is 11 months old. So, I've made a decision to concentrate on the visible parts of our house. Barnhill says, if you're lacking the motivation to do it, you don't need to be concerned. Is it really a matter of concern whether binkies or board books are scattered across the flooring?

No. A small percentage of people do not notice it. And the ones who do, I've discovered that it could cause a pleasant filtering effect on mothers of other children.

If they realize that their home isn't perfect, they can relax and believe that they don't need to be the perfect mother they watched on television.

I'm Worried About My Marriage

How do I handle my relationship? We're afraid of turning into sex-hungry zombies , who don't talk about anything other than a child.

Babies are typically great, enjoyable, and fantastic to sex killers, so if it is imperative to take on this, and you could and ought to make time for your love life. Before my son was born My husband and I kept our regular promise every Saturday nights. Also, we established a routine (this is the most important thing) that we talk about infant issues as minimally as is possible.

There are days when it seems like you've never spoken to yourself. This could quickly erode your relationship.

You can ask for a delicious postpartum meal. After he goes to bed, he open a bottle of wine, and then talks with candles. Whatever you do, be aware that it should be an ongoing routine,

It's difficult to sustain an ongoing relationship over several hours per month.

In terms of sex. It could be a difficult subject. You're probably out of breath! All you have to do when you're in bed is rest. If your child is all the day, cuddling and feeding him, during the night, he could contact your body. She suggests getting your husband to participate in physical exercise (bottle food). Also, remember to hug your husband when he's working and he's appreciated. however humble it may sound Pick the date that you'll have an affair, regardless of the time,

If you don't have any passion, it continues when you get started. Numerous young mothers find that after they've got their sex lives back in order the sex life becomes a sanctuary or something fresh. The reason they're seeking is because there's only you and your partner.

Burnout - The Big Elephant

Burnout is a common occupational symptom or syndrome that arises from inability to resolve chronic stress at work.

Burnout speaks to itself through three ways.

• Feeling exhausted or exhaustion

Excellent mental separation from the work environment or negative emotions or doubts about work

* Reduces professional effectiveness

Multitasking in the 21st Century Burnout

Today, in a world where we're constantly multitasking, it's difficult to deal with stress both at home and at work. To get more accomplished within the same time, we frequently reduce our work hours. The regular break helps our productivity by decreasing stress levels and helps us concentrate more efficiently.

Rest While Diving

Our bodies undergo routines throughout the day, where activities and energy peak, later decrease. There is a chance your energy levels are higher throughout the day, especially in the mornings and the afternoons However, by the middle of the day, you're fatigued. This is a common pattern for the majority of people, and it is important to plan for rest throughout this slowdown process as your body gets tired and requires a recharge.

It usually falls between 2 until 4 after 4. The majority of people go to work in the afternoon. There is no reason why the highest number of accidents occur during the time of day, as those who are tired do not pay attention to the things they're doing. Consequently, their bodies and minds get regenerated.

Many people don't take breaks due to fear of being unable to work. Be aware of your body. Are your eyes hurting while you stare at the computer? Do your legs feel numb after being in the same place for long periods of period of time? Do you get a headache at intervals of for 90 minutes?

There are a variety of the signals that your body's signaling to tell you when it's time for you to relax. Too often, however we disregard these signals since we think that resting reduces productivity. However, in actuality it is possible to achieve more later on. The reason is that in the span of a few minutes off from work, you can improve your mental and physical ability.

Take A Break For Results

If you make the effort and practice, you will take a physical and mental break. Select one or more of these suggestions to try during the next time you take a break.

Do some stretching; If you're as many who are long hours at their desks or at a computer, stand up off your desk every hour to walk, and then stretch your legs and arms. Also, regularly looking away from your computer can help reduce strain on your eyes.

Exercise; It improves blood flow, keeps you alert and reduces stress in the body. A change in scenery can offer you an entirely new view or solution for the issue you are facing.

Breathing exercises that are controlled involve taking slow and deep breathing through the mouth and nose. It is an excellent technique to ease anxiety, boost alertness and refresh your mind. The breathing exercises are performed while lying down. If you want to get the most benefit, attempt to complete seven or eight reps, two or three every day.

Exercise. If you can take a walk for 20 minutes or use the exercise bike or bike. The short-term workout boosts your heart rate, boosts blood flow, improves sleepiness and improves mood, boosts appetite and aids in controlling the weight.

Visualize. Visualization is an effective technique to help you enjoy the benefits of a calm atmosphere even when you can't achieve it. In the midst of a hectic day at work, lie in a chair , or lay on the floor for a few minutes to imagine yourself at the place you love to relax or relaxing in a bubbling spa tub that helps to ease tension.

Do as much as you can enjoy a good film or photo album or albums, enjoy some great music, or smell something delicious. This sends nerve signals to your brain signalling it to relax.

When you are practicing these methods be sure to follow the signals of your body. And do not let your rest dictate a routine that is rigid. If your day off is simply another thing that you have to do it won't bring what you desire. You need to rest when you're in need of the most.

Chapter 9: Everyone Is Reluctant To Admit That Having A Child

All times can cause burning out. However, motherhood isn't a rare thing particularly if you're the housewife.

There are some options to stay calm and not feel overloaded. The best way to prevent mother's exhaustion by taking handful of additional steps to make sure you don't feel as if you're a full-time caregiver all week long.

Avoid Negative People

If you have a support network that is not there to support you Your mom's anger can rapidly surface. Beware of negative people who aren't supportive of your character.

While you can't be a secretive person but you can rest assured that the vast majority of people around you are helpful and accessible to you. It is sometimes necessary to eliminate individuals who do not support the way you live your life.

There is a need for a group comprised of those who are with you and who do not make judgements about every choice that you make on behalf of you and your family.

Find Your Support System

As you would like to stay away from negative people in every way feasible, you should be around the most positive individuals feasible. If you don't have a support systemin place, build one.

Look for these people through group meetings for play or support groups at the school of your child or standing in line at the supermarket department store. Moms who have children are an excellent source because they've experienced it and are able to give you an insight of what exactly you've been through to date. You can rely on your mother and sister or any other member of your family about the difficulties you're facing.

If you don't have a solid help system, you could quickly turn into a depressed mom which can lead to exhaustion.

Put Yourself First

Most moms who visit to them first , and they'll tell you that they're just infants. If you do not look after yourself, you won't be able to be a good parent to other people. Make yourself the first priority. This doesn't mean you do not care for your family or don't want to take the right steps to your family members. Simply, it signifies that you are the primary driver of your home and you must be looked after for and provided with support, or everyone else in the family is going to be in trouble.

It is not just helpful to make the time for yourself, it can also help to prevent exhaustion of your mother.

Begin a new activity and take classes designed that are for women or ways to work from home, if you would like to explore. Little things you can take care of yourself will contribute to your wellbeing and also how your home functions and isn't a source of constant stress.

Spend Time With Your Partner

There's a reason that we refer to them as essential. Your contribution is crucial during the various stages of parenthood in a family. It's not difficult to accomplish make mistakes, you shouldn't put your relationships to the wrong end.

Whatever level of exhaustion you're feeling at the conclusion of the day, you should take time to be with your spouse. A daily chats with your spouse could bring out some of the required emotion during times when you're tired. The way you work as a team regularly on a daily routine is crucial in your outlook for the day ahead.

Just waiting for the time to unwind with your companion after a long day will help you overcome difficult moments for your parents.

Set Your Partner To Work

Family is a collective and your partner in life will be able to help to get you off the field when you feel as if your team has just destroyed you. A lot of partners are eager to assist. We can help, but we must not create a feeling of intruders as they do not have the resources to feed our children or to wear pajamas just like us.

Parents are too easily to become stuck in times of need. Mom is able to navigate her ship, since she's always there with her kids. Your partner returns home and starts feeling more relaxed, and decides not to assist because the person doesn't wish to disrupt the plans you have made.

Get rid of yourself. Spending time creating a relationship that is independent of your self will benefit both your child and partner.

Keep An Eye On Your Gadget

Recent Research study found that half a million of children polled (51 percent) believed they were frequently too distracted by their personal gadgets.

This is not just for your kids. You have your phone in your face constantly and the unneeded stress caused by all these tech-related stress

If you're looking at all the ideal parenting posts that you've seen on your feed it's just placing unrealistic expectations on yourself to be the perfect mother you envision your Facebook friends to be. Be aware that not all parents will openly share the parenting experience they have,

What's the reason? Since people spend their entire lives on social media, as well as live their lives inside a closed-door environment in a place where nobody can view their lives. I don't know about you , but this isn't my kind of person. wish to follow In short, just take a step back, show your true self.

A majority of your acquaintances will not post on social networks concerning those gruelling motherhood moments when their son's youngest is trying to flush a full package of wet wipes into the toilet, and the mother is able to scoop up an entire dozen eggs and sees what happens if he cooks them.

Stay away from devices throughout your day and you'll almost instantly be able to feel the weight lifting off your shoulders.

Stop Feeling Like You're Losing

Moms are said to be a bit of a critic inside that doesn't sleep. The inner critic causes them to doubt everything, even their parenting skills. It's not helpful for anyone, and can make one feel as if they are not doing enough as the parent you are. Make sure you let your inner critic stop! You're doing an amazing job.

It can be difficult to think that you're struggling to be a parent at the home. However, you're a great motherand can't beat the odds in parenting. You aren't required to win every parent battle.

Take off the hat of supermom and lead your life exactly as you feel.

Sleep in

Many of us think of fatigue as something women in their early years experience particularly due to sleep deprivation. Mother's fatigue can occur anytime she's not getting enough rest.

Sleep mommy. Whatever your child's age and stage of development, all children need to get a restful night's sleep.

You must also get enough sleep in order to protect your mom.

For one thing, everyone will feel content when they don't get enough sleep. Add the children and it's obvious that you need to take a time to relax and be a content mother, and ready for a fresh day full of fights between siblings as well as diaper changing and driving with kids from across the city.

Just Say No

You can't do everything, so don't even try. In the end there's no reason to feel ashamed for not achieving every request you made however it doesn't need to be.

It is important to know when you can not say yes. It is only one person, and can't do everything.

That is, put your sales of PTA cakes, making school events, or taking on the role of soccer team coach this year. Make sure to limit the number of tasks you are willing to accept to maybe one at a given time. Also, make sure you're not who is working every month. If you don't, you'll be exposed to mother exhaustion on a large magnitude.

Resist Family Over Programming

As you must be aware of when you should tell yourself no it is equally important to understand what to say when you have to decline the requests of your kids, such as soccer practice starting at 4:30 pm and then across town for your son's youngest to school the gym at 5:00 pm.

A missed schedule for your children can quickly exhaust them which is why you should know when you can not say "no" to keep your mind.

Make sure you plan at least one full day in the week when your family does not need to go anywhere other than in the evenings after school. Reduce your schedule to include some time for yourself, and you'll have less chance of burning out.

Let Your Child Do Things

Sometimes , it's more convenient to handle tasks for our kids than allow them to do it by their own. The key to raising an independent child that is responsible begins by letting them complete the task independently.

It's a breeze for your child to pour their own juice. There's a chance they'll splash a bit onto the counter, however they'll learn to pour it by themselves, while you may also take breaks while you do it.

Your child will feel satisfied with the work, even if the performance isn't ideal, and soon be ready for larger accountability. If they are able to do more on their own then the less you will have to worry about. Each little thing helps.

Take A Break

Yeah, that's right. You're due an escape from your son. Look for a Mommy Friday event that is a good fit for your needs. Find out if your family member is interested in a stand-up-and-play event for their child. They can attend to spend an hour and sometimes.

Establish a childcare cooperative that allows you to share childcare with parents who are free of cost. Find flexible and reasonable child care options. Don't forget to remember that the time you have off shouldn't be used for running around or doing household chores.

Watching for Signs of Stress

Parenting is a constant challenge that can lead to stress. The stress that comes with it can easily result in mother burning out. If you're not taking breaks, make sure you don't get sleepy and let your family members help, for example and your stress increases over time.

There is never enough time to recharge, and it can find yourself feeling overwhelmed and like things are getting too much.

Check Yourself For Signs Of Stress

You should also determine if you're suffering from the signs of depression. It's not difficult to turn into an anxious or depressed mother. Be sure to get assistance. Even though you are devoted to your kids, being a parent may be a strain on your body. Talk to your doctor with sincerity to ensure that you are the happy, healthy mother once more.

Chapter 10: The Stress Response Cycle

Your stress stage has possibly increased masses over the last few years. Most parents were laid low with the Covid-19 pandemic that beaten the globe in 2020. You may moreover have out of area cherished ones or friends to Covid, or maybe in case you failed to, you are probably struggling because of the socio-financial challenges because of the pandemic and unique geopolitical troubles.

We're going for walks extra tough than ever earlier than genuinely to make ends meet. Some folks even take on factor hustles on pinnacle of our complete-time jobs and do those after-hours to live to tell the story until the prevent of the month. Worldwide, people are in monetary problem and it's forecasted that maximum fundamental economies will fall into recession at some point of 2023. On social media, people admit to strolling 70-hour weeks an notable way to pay their bills and passing via using their marriage companions and children like ships on their way to specific ports. One can truely imagine the devastating consequences in your bodily and highbrow health, no longer to say households breaking aside if this situation have to keep for an extended length.

Burnout and the State of the World

The pandemic has moreover modified how we paintings, with many humans sincerely switching to a long manner flung paintings, blurring the street among our home and paintings lives. Our stress tiers may have extended even more due to this situation. In many times, switching off from paintings have become increasingly more complicated, and some organizations now expect their personnel to be to be had 24/7. Many oldsters even find out ourselves walking on weekends, at the same time as for some, unwell days have turn out to be a problem of the beyond.

As the sector slowly returns to a country we're capable of regard as extra "regular," we want to be aware that strain and anxiety will now not honestly disappear, in particular with all of the specific ongoing troubles we are still managing. It's even expected that Covid-19 should make a comeback and that we want to be prepared to stand extra waves in the future.

We shouldn't permit our shield down when it comes to our highbrow fitness. Surging pressure degrees and burnout can simplest enlarge the restoration phase if we do not prioritize our highbrow fitness and nicely-being.

We're usually advised we want to research time control to control our strain stages, but you may actually need to recognition more on coping with your electricity stages than some time, specially as regards to burnout. Your strength levels will determine what you acquire at the give up of the day. Getting some aspect finished is difficult at the equal time as you're burned out and exhausted. Your productiveness will decrease, and you could come to be much less effective in all regions of your life.

What Is Burnout?

While burnout can creep up on you, you can understand the signs and symptoms and signs and symptoms when they hit you complete-on. You can try to hold going with the resource of ingesting excessive portions of espresso and power drinks or ingesting sugary and fatty ingredients. However, quickly you will be emotionally, bodily, and mentally exhausted. This can occur if you have been uncovered to excessive strain for an prolonged period. You is probably feeling beaten and prefer you can't address the regular desires for your non-public and expert life.

For many humans, the experience down the slippery slope to burnout starts when they have unmeetable dreams and desires. They get to a level where their brains can't cope with it to any quantity in addition, and a few component has to provide.

They emerge as increasingly irritated till they supply into melancholy. They get trapped in a cycle amongst hating their jobs and feeling they can not depart as they need the coins to raise their youngsters and pay their bills.

Long-term burnout is likewise stressful due to the fact it could motive adjustments for your body and make you extra liable to infection. Therefore, it's miles tremendous to cope with burnout as speedy as possible whilst you recognize the symptoms and signs and symptoms.

If you are taking observe of the early signs and symptoms, you could prevent a prime breakdown.

Symptoms

Burnout has some painful and tiring physical symptoms, like exhaustion—you have got were given to tug your self out of bed each morning and slightly make it there. On days just like the ones, you're happy you are the use of public transport, as you might not additionally be able to be aware about the usage of a vehicle. Your mind handiest wakes up after numerous cups of coffee.

You can also be sick all of the time. You pick out up every single contamination the youngsters carry from university, making you even greater confused as you grow to be increasingly more unpopular for taking such a lot of unwell days.

Burnout also can purpose you to sleep poorly and wake up numerous instances a night. Sometimes you could war to go to sleep. You're ingesting extra than ever and counting on sugar and coffee to get you through the long days, which ends up in weight advantage.

You have common headaches and muscle ache, which makes it even extra of a drag to get thru the day.

The emotional fallout of burnout can also get you down. Self-doubt may additionally want to make you enjoy like a failure at the same time as matters begin to pass incorrect at paintings. The reactions of coworkers regularly do no longer assist, mainly even as humans start gambling the blame undertaking, and no person desires to take private obligation. Before you come to be too pessimistic and cynical and take your frustrations out on them, recall that your colleagues may additionally have out of place their motivation for their jobs because of burnout. Burned out personnel often lose their feelings of achievement, which decreases their pride within the place of business.

If you are an extrovert, one of the signs and symptoms and signs and symptoms and signs additionally may be which you start to isolate your self increasingly more from other people. You can also additionally discover yourself procrastinating at artwork and home and taking all the time to get topics carried out.

Reasons for Burnout

There are several motives and forms of burnout, and also you need to realise a few component approximately those to shield yourself from burning out or get over it.

The reasons for burnout within the workplace are obvious, but it keeps to reveal up, and employees and their employers pay the fee.

Some of the primary reasons embody unmanageable workloads and unfair remedy. In many offices, the excessive performers and hard personnel frequently emerge as with the majority of the artwork and responsibilities. People can emerge as sick from pressure, but they may be despite the fact that expected to keep maximum of the weight, at the identical time as inefficient personnel on occasion get to cruise at the side of out severe results. This isn't always constantly the case, but it is an awful lot less complex for unmotivated employees to cover in departments in which it's far anticipated that one or efficient personnel have to supply others.

This form of unfair remedy can result in or get worse burnout. If you are a excessive performer, you are regularly predicted to keep up this tempo, and if you make one unlucky mistakes, it is able to be held in the direction of you. However, your underperforming coworkers maintain making mistakes with out elevating eyebrows.

If you find out yourself strolling in an area like this, do not forget that it's miles in no way really worth sacrificing your health to fulfill the unreasonable demands of someone else, which include your managers at paintings. When your fitness is affected, getting it decrease back to the kingdom it emerge as earlier than is probably tough, specially when you have to keep strolling on this environment. Ultimately, it's not low-priced to sacrifice your fitness to vicinity massive money into a person else's pocket. If your artwork environment is toxic, your first rate desire may be to find out a way out as quick as feasible. Or you could decide out of your exploitative work subculture via quite quitting.

Quiet Quitting

This term has lengthy long long past into drift pretty presently and describes a today's way of managing administrative center burnout.

When you "quiet prevent," because it's referred to as inside the famous communicate, you're not absolutely quitting your assignment, but you are doing fine the fundamentals in choice to on foot the so-referred to as extra mile. Basically, you nice do enough to hold your task. This term only appears to had been round for the purpose that August final yr, which sincerely indicates you what a severe trouble burnout has grow to be.

While some humans regard it as a bad concept that would value you your challenge or be lousy on your lengthy-term profession, others see it as ideally fitted and can advocate people had been doing this for years. You may additionally moreover have had coworkers who refuse to do greater than what's indicated of their way description.

Those individuals who're slightly older and characteristic had a poisonous art work ethic (you want to artwork difficult even when you have to sacrifice your non-public health) drilled into us can also furthermore conflict with the idea of quiet quitting. However, it's miles famous among more youthful generations who refuse to bow proper down to poisonous place of job cultures.

Think or say approximately it what you want, but quiet quitting can also want to prevent burnout or assist you get over burnout. Burnout is often the end result of cultural expectations as opposed to actual paintings necessities. For instance, a few employers have to anticipate their personnel to be to be had and obedient always. You throw off those expectancies in case you're a quiet quitter.

Quiet quitting is a useful technique in case you sense trapped for your pastime.

It's an first-rate method while you cannot break out your stressor. It does now not always suggest now not doing all your technique, however it could sincerely endorse changing your method for your paintings and that you do now not have to burn your self out for the sake of hard work. For example, you may move from taking on huge portions of extra artwork and working the least bit hours to truly sticking for your everyday hours. Remember, the next day is each other day. Quiet quitting may also moreover contain growing thick pores and skin. The idea is that it permits you to dismiss managers and coworkers who place needless strain on you, e.G., individuals who need to get the undertaking finished at any price, regularly due to the fact they may be regularly not worried in having to do it themselves.

When Is Quiet Quitting For You?

Quiet quitting might be for you if you're the form of character who has placed a fantastic deal of strive into their paintings, and plenty of your self-worth is likewise derived from the form of device you do. For example, your vanity gets a lift even as you're promoted to a manipulate function.

In this situation, it is going to be better on your intellectual health to detach your self confidence out of your unreasonable working conditions. You're loads extra treasured than any contribution you are making at artwork.

At first, you will likely experience a experience of loss or maybe disappointment. However, fast you can discover which means in new sports activities after you're capable of get the concept out of your head which you have to commit your whole being to your manner.

Confusing or changing paintings responsibilities also can add fuel to the burnout fireplace. Just when you have the address on one venture, the method changes, or greater obligations get dumped on you. Employees are then held accountable for becoming harassed with this manner of running and not keeping up with the multiple modifications. If your administrative center talents this way, it's far in all likelihood splendid to defend yourself in competition to burnout via growing thick pores and skin.

If you're burned out, you've got likely professional a lack of guide and proper verbal exchange out of your managers. This can bypass hand-in-hand with complex paintings responsibilities. Just even as you expect you're at the right route, you get driven off in each different course. If you've got a manager who is simply interested in appearing and squeezing the very last little little little bit of workout consultation of you to advantage a few issue, do not expect them to understand at the same time as you are experiencing a fitness or circle of relatives disaster.

Hectic lessen-off date strain can also push you over the closing date thing. It's crucial to keep off toward this, as your health will continuously be greater important. Remember that at the equal time as you're replaceable at art work, your own family and loved ones can't replace you.

Types of Burnout

There are genuinely 3 varieties of burnout with notable reasons:

•Overload burnout generally happens while you're beyond pushed in your pursuit of success. You do no longer mind risking your fitness and private lifestyles to achieve success at your process.

•Under-challenged burnout takes place at the same time as you are bored at your activity, and you may distance yourself from it and keep away from responsibilities. It's possible there are not any boom opportunities or possibilities for gaining knowledge of and schooling. Beware of corporations that do not spend money on their personnel.

•Neglect burnout might be the saddest kind. You experience helpless and incapable of preserving up along side your duties. This can also be connected to imposter syndrome, in which you will doubt your abilties, competencies, or accomplishments.

The Difference Between Burnout, Stress, Fatigue, and Exhaustion

Interestingly, burnout have end up to begin with appeared as a syndrome that resulted from workplace strain now not being managed successfully. Its three important signs and signs and symptoms have been said to be feelings of exhaustion, an advanced mental distance out of your system, and feeling increasingly horrible toward your hobby, which induced you becoming an lousy lot much less green. It became said that burnout must no longer be used to provide an explanation for reviews in high-quality life areas.

Many corporations are taking burnout more severely now that it's regarded as a place of business crisis. It's vital to apprehend that burnout isn't similar to strain, and you cannot repair it by means of running fewer hours, taking an extended excursion, or slowing down in present day. When you are under stress, you still battle to address stress. Once you are burned out, you have got given up all desire of overcoming your limitations. You begin to be given as actual with that each one your efforts are vain and that you'll be dropping a while irrespective of what you do. You cannot even meet the smallest duties or maybe doing a small mission seems like mountaineering a big mountain.

It may additionally additionally be which you're fatigued. You might be feeling inclined and worn-out, and plenty of human beings expect that fatigue and tiredness are the same issue. However, there's a good sized difference. Fatigue is constant and can final for years, however you can get better quite rapid from being worn-out. Your fatigue is probably physical, highbrow, or even because of a combination of things.

As a quit end result of our demanding contemporary-day way of existence, we're all liable to falling prey to a number of the ones factors. You have a life-style of staying up overdue, eating loads of alcohol and caffeine, and also you need consuming pizza each other night time time of the week. You're definitely now not a fan of healthful food. After all, you are no longer sincerely living your life at the same time as you are ingesting leaves like a rabbit. Your frame is too tired to stress it to do exercise, and also you walk simplest even as you truly ought to.

Your process has grow to be a nightmare of long shifts, 7-day art work weeks, and not to mention boredom. Just the concept of going there can be making you worrying and depressed. However, the situation can nonetheless be remedied in case you studies a few stress manage techniques and artwork on improving your manner of existence.

Exhaustion is a shorter-lived form of fatigue that also can get you down emotionally, bodily, and mentally. However, if periods of exhaustion building up, you can come to be fatigued after which burned out.

So how do you truly inform the difference amongst exhaustion, fatigue, and burnout? The best way is to see how lengthy it takes you to get better.

If all it takes is a remarkable night time time's sleep, a nutritious meal, and a relaxing shower, then you definitely definately're likely suffering from tiredness.

If you can get going again after a two-week tour targeted on de-stressing and unplugging, you be troubled by using exhaustion. However, it'd take you a couple of months to conquer fatigue.

If you're burned out, the situation may take longer to repair. It will depend on your popular state of affairs and also how lengthy you have were given been burned out. It should assist hundreds if you could have a have a look at a few coping techniques for burnout, like running towards meditation.

An exquisite manner to manipulate the ones types of situations is to music into your very personal dreams. Look at your artwork-life balance and exercising some healthful techniques to unwind. It's moreover vital to make certain you get enough sleep.

Be in touch together together with your feelings and try to manipulate them to the exceptional of your capability. Emotional or intellectual stress can purpose you to behave erratically even in case you're now not physically worn-out. Keep in contact along with your circle of relatives and create a healthful help network.

How Stress Affects Your Body

Most oldsters recognize pressure is terrible in your highbrow fitness, but it may additionally be terrible for the rest of your frame, out of your disturbing in your reproductive device.

Central Nervous and Endocrine Systems

You've possibly heard of your combat-or-flight reaction. Well, strain can cause this reaction, it is managed via the usage of your number one disturbing system (CNS).

When you experience forced, your mind sends signals via your body. The stress hormones on your frame will boom, and you may enjoy this as your coronary coronary heart will beat quicker.

Your apprehensive system will move again to regular as soon as the strain has handed, but when you have continual strain, your body will live in a defensive reaction. This can supply you seeking out strategies to eliminate the horrific emotions. It can be tough to stay faraway from alcohol or capsules or gather for consolation foods which can be greater often than now not bad. Or you can just no longer experience like eating the least bit.

Respiratory and Cardiovascular Systems

When you are confused, you could find out respiratory extra tough, specifically in case you be bothered with the aid of a situation like allergies, chronic bronchitis, or emphysema.

The greater adrenaline for your frame might also additionally even boom blood waft, at the same time as your coronary coronary coronary heart rate and blood pressure will boom as your frame pumps greater blood to your coronary coronary heart, specific crucial organs, and muscle groups to get them organized for action.

If you are constantly compelled for a long time, your coronary coronary coronary heart will have to art work more difficult, that could push your blood pressure up and could even cause you to have a coronary coronary coronary heart assault or stroke.

Digestive System

If you continuously have stomach pain, bloating, nausea, constipation, and diarrhea, it is able to be because of strain. It can also purpose irritable bowel syndrome (IBS) and get worse it.

Stress also can purpose you to increase type 2 diabetes or worsen if you already be afflicted with the useful resource of it.

Muscular System

We've all had this painful revel in. You're already harassed, rolling spherical at night because you cannot sleep, and your muscle mass disturbing up. Painful neck, shoulder, and yet again pain is mostly a forestall result of pressure. Have you been sitting in one characteristic at work too prolonged because you need to satisfy annoying cut-off dates? That ought to provide an purpose behind your decrease lower back ache.

The muscular tissues will typically loosen up as quickly as the pressure passes, however you may revel in pain for longer durations of time when you have chronic stress.

Reproductive System

Stress may want to make you mentally and physically worn-out, and you can find out your self warding off intercourse. In women who be afflicted by way of premenstrual syndrome or PMS, your signs and symptoms and signs may additionally worsen, and your periods need to get heavier and greater painful. They may want to even emerge as bizarre. When you're having a annoying month, you can generally find out that your period and PMS are worse than during instances you aren't careworn.

If you are going thru menopause, your symptoms additionally can be worse in the path of a stressful time due to an boom in hormone degrees.

You can also war to get pregnant, and strain can complicate being pregnant.

Chronic pressure can cause men's testosterone ranges to drop, effect their sperm ranges and cause troubles like impotence, erectile sickness, or infections inside the prostate or testes.

Immune System

Chronic stress will weaken your immune system, and you can find it takes you longer to get better when you get sick or grow to be injured. You'll additionally seize viruses much less complicated, consisting of colds, flu, and Covid-19.

How to Break Your Stress Cycle

These days, it is now common to experience like we are in a everyday america of the usa of pressure. Stressors are all round us, and loads of us in no manner entire our strain cycles. A strain cycle may have many levels, and we whole one while our our bodies examine we are constant after facing chance.

The chance is that if we do not confront our pressure, our our our bodies will stay in a everyday kingdom of activation with prolonged blood strain, placing us at a higher threat of developing coronary coronary heart illness and digestion issues. Therefore, completing a stress cycle could be very vital for our health.

When it includes the pressure cycle, it's far critical to recognise that there are definitely one among a kind stages:

1.   Stage one is at the same time as the out of doors stressor or triggering occasion takes location. For instance, a person says some factor to you that makes you unhappy.

2.   At level , your senses start to understand a few detail has lengthy past wrong and deliver statistics for your amygdala (this is the part of your thoughts

that strategies facts like worry and anger). When your amygdala is activated, a sign goes in your hypothalamus and pituitary gland, which might be chargeable for keeping the stableness in your body.

3.   When you benefit level 3, your sympathetic concerned device is activated, and your frame is going into combat or flight reaction mode. It's then that your coronary coronary heart charge starts offevolved going up, and your immune and digestive structures are negatively affected.

four.   At degree four, you may begin to be conscious the pressure. Your signs and symptoms, which includes expanded coronary coronary heart charge and frame aches, will now become greater essential than at degree three. You may also furthermore now start demanding approximately how well you are managing strain and experience involved and traumatic.

5.   Stage 5, the final diploma of the cycle, has to do with the manner you address your pressure. You're beginning to search for techniques to deal with your pain. However, if you manipulate it in a maladaptive manner, you may absolutely growth your strain. These techniques must paintings within the brief term, however you can emerge as with hundreds worse troubles inside the long term. These strategies, which might be moreover poisonous in your highbrow fitness, can encompass the usage of tablets and/or alcohol, continuously checking your cell phone, or overworking. If you use the ones strategies, you could find out your self in a hyper-aroused country and more stressed out than in advance than.

How To Complete the Stress Cycle

Getting at least hours of bodily hobby in step with week is important. This can encompass on foot, swimming, dancing, or a few issue which you enjoy doing that gets you moving.

Creativity also can help you entire the cycle. Do a few issue you enjoy, whether or now not it's miles writing, gardening, or cooking. Laughing is an clean manner to release bottled-up feelings. Watch a funny movie or visit some buddies who usually make you chortle.

You also can release pressure through deep breathing wearing sports along with yoga and tai chi.

One of the maximum important topics is making sure you get enough relaxation, as a excellent night's sleep can help your frame get over annoying activities.

Physical affection and call from a loved you may in reality make you experience regular. Crying is every one-of-a-kind manner your frame can release pressure, and you have to in no manner strive repressing your tears.

The Difference Between Stress and Stressors

You want to understand the difference among pressure and stressors to have the ability to finish the strain reaction cycle and recover from burnout.

Stress

Stress releases hormones on your frame, mainly cortisol and adrenaline, which positioned your frame into fight or flight mode. This is on the same time as you war to make alternatives, and your immune system and digestion are already affected. If you've got been a part of early mankind, it manner you in all likelihood could have been capable of escape a predator, but in our cutting-edge worldwide, it only cripples your desire-making capability. And as stated earlier than, if this includes on for a long time, your fitness will take a knock.

Stressors

Most humans will see pressure as some difficulty in their lives out of doors of themselves that they can not manage. For most people, this will be artwork and coins. So, the things that reason pressure are "stressors," even as "pressure" is your response to the ones stressors.

Stress will always be there, and some of the time, you can not be able to keep away from your stressors. But you may control your response to them. This can embody wholesome coping mechanisms like meditation.

Interactive Element: Burnout Self-Test

The self-evaluation explores the risk of burnout via way of the usage of searching at exhaustion, depersonalization, and private achievement. The device can offer you with a few useful notion, but you need to not use it as a systematic diagnostic technique. At every question, suggest the rating that corresponds for your reaction. Add up your scores for the sections after which examine your outcomes with the interpretation at the lowest of the assessment.

Questions

Never

A Few Times a Year

Once a Months

A Few Times steady with Month

Once a Week

A Few Times constant with Week

Every Day

Section A

0

1

2

3

four

five

6

My mission drains me emotionally.

I want to make some of strive as soon as I artwork with people.

My interest frustrates me.

I experience my artwork is destroying my spirit.

I revel in I art work too hard.

I experience I'm on the forestall of my tether.

It stresses me too much to artwork with humans.

Score – SECTION A

Section B

zero

1

2

three

4

5

6

I address my coworkers in an impersonal way, almost as even though they may be items.

I'm already worn-out once I arise in the morning and need to go to paintings.

It appears to me that my colleagues are preserving me accountable for some of their issues.

I do no longer care approximately what takes location to my colleagues or group.

I do not have patience after an afternoon at art work.

I have emerge as insensitive closer to humans within the administrative center.

It feels as even though this project is making me uncaring.

Score – SECTION B

Section C

0

1

2

three

4

five

6

I experience that I accomplish worthwhile topics in my assignment.

I am lively.

It's clean for me to apprehend what my coworkers revel in.

I can look after my coworker's issues effectively.

I am able to address troubles at art work very lightly.

I sense that I clearly have a extraordinary have an effect on on human beings.

I can create a comfortable ecosystem with my coworkers.

I am refreshed as soon as I even have spent time with my coworkers.

Total rating – SECTION C

Interpretation of Results

Compare your consequences to the listing beneath.

Section A - Burnout

You can degree your stage of burnout regular with the following effects:

30 and over: High-degree burnout

Between 18 and 29: Moderate burnout

17 or a good deal less: Low-degree burnout

Section B: Depersonalization (Loss of empathy)

12 and higher: High-diploma burnout

Between 6 and eleven: Moderate burnout

5 or a bargain much less: low-degree burnout

Section C: Personal Achievement (Are you demotivated and revel in like you aren't carrying out some thing?)

More than forty: Low-stage burnout

Between 34 and 39: Moderate burnout

33 or a extraordinary deal much less: High-degree burnout

If you've got got accomplished a immoderate score within the first sections and a low score within the remaining segment, you may be experiencing burnout.

Remember that the test isn't a scientific evaluation. You nevertheless want to are searching out advice from a systematic physician or intellectual fitness expert in case you need assist with strain control or if you think you may be dealing with burnout.

Key Takeaways

•Burnout need to creep up on you, but you will recognize the symptoms after they virtually hit you. Many come to be emotionally, mentally, and bodily exhausted after which attempt to keep going by using manner of consuming dangerous meals and consuming immoderate quantities of espresso and strength drinks.

•Long-term burnout can also make you more susceptible to contamination. You can get ill more effects, however inside the long term, you can additionally boom chronic conditions which includes excessive blood strain and coronary heart problems.

•The signs and symptoms of burnout can be painful and tiring and include exhaustion, not unusual contamination, and disrupted sleep.

•You can start feeling like a failure at the same time as things skip wrong at paintings. You might also turn out to be no longer searching for to go to paintings in any respect. If you figure in a poisonous environment, "quiet quitting" is probably an option if you're no longer able to depart your way.

•Burnout also can purpose you to procrastinate at paintings and at domestic. You may also revel in along with you sincerely do no longer have the electricity to get subjects completed, and you may find yourself constantly distracted, e.G., via manner of spending time on social media even as your thoughts isn't always capable of recognition.

•Unmanageable workloads and unfair treatment are some of the precept motives for burnout within the place of job. The high performers and difficult employees regularly become with the majority in their paintings and duties in poisonous artwork environments, in particular in which there is insufficient manage ability.

•Confusing or constantly changing artwork responsibilities also can add to burnout. For instance, really at the identical time as you are used to best tactics at work, they change, or greater paintings gets dumped on you.

•In artwork environments with burnout, there is usually a loss of manual from managers and confusing paintings duties.

•Hectic deadlines can also make contributions to burnout.

•People who be afflicted by overload burnout are normally parents which can be very pushed to collect success. These humans do no longer thoughts risking their health and private lives to gain fulfillment at their jobs.

•Under-challenged burnout typically takes place to individuals who are bored at their jobs and do no longer have opportunities for reading and schooling.

•People who be via imposter syndrome and doubt their abilities and accomplishments can end up sufferers of overlook approximately burnout. This might also want to reason them to sense helpless and as though they are not able to keep up with their responsibilities.

•It is important to apprehend that burnout isn't always just like pressure. You cannot repair burnout thru way of going for walks fewer hours, slowing down, or taking an extended excursion.

•You can manipulate your burnout, fatigue, and exhaustion with the aid of way of way of tuning into your very personal goals. Think cautiously approximately your place of job stability and recollect wholesome techniques that will help you unwind. Make fine you get enough sleep.

•You can be feeling susceptible and worn-out, however it is essential to realize that fatigue and tiredness aren't the identical issue. The distinction is that you could experience constantly fatigued, that could even very last for years. When you're tired, you could generally get higher rapid, even after an exceptional night time time's sleep.

•It's now not uncommon to sense constantly burdened, as pressure is all spherical us, and we are able to discover it in all components of our lives. Many human beings in no way entire their strain cycles, which can be very vital, as you need to complete your pressure cycle on your body to enjoy secure and studies that it is no longer in chance.

•Completing a pressure cycle is vital on your fitness. If we do now not confront our pressure, our bodies will live in a steady u . S

. Of activation, and we must boom all varieties of fitness problems, like excessive blood pressure, coronary heart troubles, and digestion issues.

•Exercise allow you to a exceptional deal in terms of completing your pressure cycle. Do something you enjoy or that receives you shifting, together with swimming, dancing, or taking walks. Not every person enjoys going to the health club, so exercising out of doors is flawlessly quality, as an example, if you want to move taking walks.

•Creative sports activities activities additionally will allow you to entire your pressure cycle. Do a few component amusing to you, which encompass writing, painting, baking a cake, or something activities you revel in.

•Make incredible you get enough sleep, as sleep is instrumental in supporting you get over strain, fatigue, tiredness, exhaustion, and burnout.

•Most human beings will see strain as some thing outdoor of themselves that they cannot manipulate, together with paintings and coins. These stressors and your reaction to them are the stress you experience.

•Stress will continuously be a big part of existence, and additionally you could now not be able to avoid your stressors. That is why learning to control your reaction to them is critical.

Chapter 11: Move Your Body

I enjoy pressured as I placed my yoga mat down after an prolonged day at art work. I struggle to set up my mind and feel as though I without a doubt need to interrupt out from myself. Of direction, that is now not viable, however exercising is the subsequent splendid detail for me.

The heat air within the room opens up my lungs as I breathe outside and inside, loosening up my traumatic muscle organizations. My headache disappears almost right away. As I whole every pose and end up extra privy to my breath, my mind will become quiet. I experience my coronary coronary heart beating and slowing down as I breathe, developing stillness. My muscle mass enjoy strong and re-energized. Sweat drips down my frame, and I enjoy gratitude for my mind, frame, and breath.

When I in the long run open my eyes, I had forgotten that I changed into ever stressed.

My thoughts is comfortable and happy. I'm at peace with the area.

The exciting feeling you enjoy after a exercise is a end stop result of your frame completing its strain cycle. You've managed to reveal off your flight-or-fight reaction, and you're stable all over again.

The Benefits of Exercise

Exercise should have many benefits to your bodily fitness. Many people warfare to stick to exercising routines that we do now not revel in, so the trick is to locate a few issue you enjoy doing.

Getting Started With Exercise

It's never too beyond because of begin exercising, but you want to take it gradual if you have now not performed any workout for a long term or communicate for your medical doctor to ensure your fitness is right enough to start exercise.

Exercise has extended-term benefits like decreasing your threat of developing coronary coronary heart ailment and diabetes and strengthening your bones and muscle companies. Still, while you honestly get into it, you'll additionally find out a few useful quick-term blessings.

It let you manage your weight. Now, do not rush out, buy a scale, and weigh your self each day. This is not a healthy manner of living. You'll find which you obviously lose a few weight even as doing exercising. Even if it's miles not a number of weight, you can emerge as being healthier, and you may revel in extra wholesome.

If you're a smoker, exercising also can assist you stop. It can assist reduce cravings and withdrawal symptoms and signs and symptoms and symptoms and restriction your weight advantage after quitting.

Exercise is also a fantastic mood booster. When you exercise, your frame releases chemical substances as a manner to enhance your mood and make you experience cushty. The strain of the day will disappear, and you additionally face a lower chance of growing depression.

Simple Exercises To Get You Moving

When it involves fitness, everybody should begin on the begin. Even high-quality-healthy human beings and expert athletes had to start from scratch extended in the beyond once they were all inexperienced youngsters. If you have not exercised in a long time, or you're most effective starting now, amateur exercising workout routines are an extraordinary manner to introduce your body to workout. If you've got were given any fitness problems, you need to see your physician for a physical and get their recommendation earlier than you begin exercise. Remember, you want to be secure at the same time as you workout, due to the truth the intention is to benefit your health and no longer damage it.

Your exceptional bet is to gather a weekly exercising application that focuses on special components of health, for you that will help you get in shape rapid and reduce your danger of harm. Focus on those five areas to make improvement faster on the subject of your fitness and staying energy: muscular strength, cardiovascular staying power, flexibility, muscular persistence, and frame composition.

www.ingramcontent.com/pod-product-compliance
Lightning Source LLC
Chambersburg PA
CBHW062139020426
42335CB00013B/1260